Nothing has shaped me and my view  of pregnancy, loss, birth, and raising c than a metaphor, it's an altar. With has reclaimed childbirth as a profounc partnership with our Creator. *Holy Lal* only to experience an empowered and Christ-centred childbirth, but to encounter the living God in that experience.

Sarah Bessey
author of *Jesus Feminist* and *Out of Sorts*

Holy Labor is a much-needed positive Christian account of childbirth. Aubry Smith's appreciation that "we understand God better when we understand childbirth better" is spot on. *Holy Labor* is a thoughtful guide to approaching birth with wisdom, grace, and yes, even joy! A must-read for expectant and experienced mothers, as well as anyone seeking a deeper understanding for how the love of God shows up in the meaningful labor of childbirth.

Courtney B. Ellis
pastor for spiritual formation at Presbyterian Church
of the Master; writer at CourtneyBEllis.com

As an experienced childbirth educator and doula, Aubry G. Smith has provided a much-needed book on the topic of childbirth from a Christian perspective. She does so in a way that is both biblically and theologically anchored while being extremely practical. Her personal vignettes lace through the book and accentuate vital spiritual practices that deepen one's faith. I cannot wait to refer this book to the expectant moms I know!

Diane J. Chandler, PhD
associate professor, Regent University School of Divinity;
author of *Christian Spiritual Formation: An Integrative
Approach to Personal and Relational Wholeness*

Holy Labor

HOW CHILDBIRTH
SHAPES A
WOMAN'S SOUL

Holy Labor

HOW CHILDBIRTH

SHAPES A

WOMAN'S SOUL

AUBRY G. SMITH

KIRKDALE PRESS

Holy Labor: How Childbirth Shapes A Woman's Soul

Copyright 2016 Aubry G. Smith

Kirkdale Press, 1313 Commercial St., Bellingham, WA 98225
Visit us at KirkdalePress.com or follow us on Twitter at @KirkdalePress

Print ISBN 9781577997382
Digital ISBN 9781577997399

Kirkdale Editorial: Abigail Stocker
Cover Design: Christine Gerhart
Back Cover Design: Liz Donovan
Typesetting: ProjectLuz.com

For my children—Breckon, Kian, and Eden—in whose births I've seen the glory of God.

And in memory of my mother, Pamela Grace Lambert, who labored with God to bring me life.

Contents

Contents

A Biblical Perspective of Childbirth

"The Most Painful Experience in the World"

A strange feeling came over me during my Cell Biology lecture one October afternoon during my final semester of college. I hadn't missed my period yet—it was due to come in four days—but somehow I knew it wasn't going to come this month. When the lecture ended, I hurried to the nearest store to buy a pregnancy test. A few minutes later, the strange feeling was confirmed: I was pregnant.

I felt I was shifting—not just in the newly joined cells implanting in my uterus but in everything that made up my life. I was growing a new life in my body and preparing to bring it into the world. I could sense the significance, but I had no words for the experience. I was finishing my undergraduate degree in biology, but the scientific language I had learned about pregnancy and birth wasn't quite sufficient. I was double majoring in Christian studies, but none of the theology books I had read discussed pregnancy or childbirth in depth. Searching for vocabulary and meaning, I spent those months deeply introspectively, my hand on my growing belly in wonder. Despite my nausea, sciatica, and insomnia, the pregnancy was full of excitement and anticipation for both my husband and me. Would our baby be a boy or girl? What would our child's personality be like—did these kicks and rolls give us any hints? How would our lives be changed, expanded, and enriched by this little human? Pregnancy and parenthood were bursting with possibility.

However, my thoughts concerning childbirth were different. If someone had asked me how I felt about childbirth, I would have said, "It's the most painful experience in the world!" The only way I knew to view birth was through the lens of fear and pain. Veteran moms shared their war stories of excruciating contractions, hours of pushing, and emergency cesareans. Most women I knew chose an epidural, certain they could not handle the physical pain of labor. My own mother, who gave birth to five children, patted my hand and said, "Ask for Demerol. It's *fabulous*." Everything I heard about childbirth was based in fear and the expectation of unbearable pain. These war stories confirmed my beliefs about childbirth: It's the worst experience in the world, and a mother's job is merely to survive it.

While not against pain relief (I'm no martyr!), I felt uneasy about this common understanding—that women could not bear what God designed their bodies to do. I fumbled as I tried to merge theological and biological information. It seemed a given that God had cursed Eve and her daughters with pain in childbirth for her sin—isn't that what Genesis 3:16 says? Who can escape God's judgment? I felt as if I should forego any pain relief during labor to avoid somehow thwarting God's judgment-related purposes for childbirth.

Filled with dread for my due date, I decided on a medication-free birth, determined to grit my teeth and bear the pain to please God somehow. My first labor conformed to my expectations: My first childbirth experience was frightening and painful. I began telling my own birth war story to expectant moms, assuming all mothers were doomed to bear the agony of childbirth. In my conversations with expectant moms I perpetuated the narrative of an angry God inflicting horrific pain on women, possibly sealing *their* expectations—and experiences—of childbirth with the same dread and resignation.

Childbirth in the Life of the Church

Most women will become mothers, and many sense that from the moment of conception all the way through parenting, every aspect of their mothering *matters*. It's a trend highlighted in recent years by increasingly extravagant birth-related celebrations in the West. The budding traditions of elaborate pregnancy announcements, clever gender-reveal parties, baby showers, blessingways (mother blessings), and whimsical photography of newborns and new parents signal more than that too many women are on Pinterest. These milestones—the discovery of a pregnancy, the revelation of the gender, and the transformation of a man and woman into a father and mother—are life-changing moments that *should be* celebrated.

The church should embrace these milestones and find meaningful ways to honor and celebrate birth. Beyond community celebrations, though, the church should consider the profound implications of transformation, new birth, and raising children—both literal and metaphorical—within the fold of faith. In general, the church has little to say to women preparing for childbirth. While women can bring their medical concerns to trained caregivers, where should expectant mothers take their fears, their desire to honor God in birth, and their questions about how to view a God who created childbirth this way? While resources on biblical parenting abound, there are virtually no resources for Christian women who want to explore the significance of childbirth through a biblical lens.

Instead, books—primarily by New Age or secular birth experts—teach them to find strength within themselves, look to their inner goddess, and form a cosmic union with the universe. While Christians recoil at such teachings, the *practical* birth advice given in many of these books is sound. Women who follow such advice often report reduced or no pain in childbirth as well as a satisfying, and even spiritual, transformative birth experience. While secular and New Age birth experts cannot promise easy labor for all women, they *do* promise more dignity and peace for the laboring mother than current Christian assumptions about childbirth provide.

Does the Bible have nothing to say about facing fear, suffering for the sake of bringing someone life, finding purpose in pain, experiencing peace, or childbirth in general? How should Christians view birth?

Childbirth and Theology

Throughout the history of the church, theology has been predominantly written and taught by men who overlooked the significant and prevalent theme of childbirth in Scripture. Worse, church leaders of the past taught that the childbirth experience was God's judgment on women. The church often marginalizes today's discussion about childbirth as a women's issue, perhaps derisively so by those who have relegated it to feminist theology. Thus there is no robust theology of childbirth within the church.

Childbirth should be brought in from the margins. Every man and woman participated in childbirth as a child, and a majority of women have or will give birth. Men participate in conception, in supporting women throughout pregnancy, and, in the West, as supporters in childbirth. Men's lives are also transformed through childbirth when they emerge as fathers. Childbirth is not exclusively a women's issue. It's a *human* issue.

Childbirth is theological—we understand God better when we understand childbirth better. The Bible is replete with rich birth-related descriptions of our God—who created birth, who co-creates with humans in conception and childbirth, who gave birth to and nursed Israel, who opens and closes wombs, and who himself participated in childbirth as a baby. Our theology concerning childbirth should cause us to ask questions about what we believe about God. Do we believe he is cursing women with pain again and again as a continued judgment for Eve's sin? Is he pleased with birth? Angry? A helper in childbirth?

With its writhing and moaning and grunting, childbirth certainly seems excruciating and irredeemable, save for the baby on the other side. But many women from various cultures and times have a different view and experience of the power of birth. Many Christian mothers have experienced the same transformative power, but without a biblical perspective on birth they are left without clear language for this important part of their lives. In the process of creating a new life in their wombs, God is also re-creating the heart of the mother as she carries, delivers, and nurtures her child. The lack of biblical insight into the process of childbirth has left a void for many Christian women, who have little framework with which to process the effect of this extraordinary event on their souls.

The void created by the lack of biblical discussion on childbirth is felt not only in the delivery ward but also in the church. Echoing the attitudes of many Christians, one popular pastor said, "God has revealed himself to us in the Bible *pervasively* as King, not Queen, and as Father, not Mother. The second person of the Trinity is revealed as the eternal Son ... God has given Christianity a *masculine feel.*"[1] Since women bear the image of God *equally* with men, the church needs a reminder of the unique ways that women reflect God's nature, character, and person. God did not create Adam in his image and then come up with nonimaging, feminine traits for Eve. She represents God *together* with Adam as they both bear the image of God. A church that has merely a "masculine feel" is not one that fully represents the God we image.

The theme of childbirth in the Bible, which we will explore, undeniably shows that women represent God by giving birth just as much as men represent God in their masculine roles. Recovering a biblical notion of childbirth can help us worship God more fully as we seek less of a "masculine feel" or even a "feminine feel" in the church. Instead, the church should be ever transforming into the image of Christ (2 Cor 3:18), who is "the image of the invisible God" (Col 1:15). Childbirth provides one avenue for women to reflect God.

The birth of my third child, Eden, proved to me that childbirth could indeed be a significant spiritual experience that reflects God, honors his creative power, and affects the soul of the mother.

During my pregnancy with Eden I was engaged in intense prayer and worship, overcame fear through the power and peace of the Holy Spirit, and sought the counsel of Scripture (as well as birth professionals) on birth. Instead of my midwives and my husband treating me as a damsel in distress or a medical case to be managed, they treated me as a strong deliverer of life, a valorous woman. I experienced pain during the birth, but it was not unbearable or pointless. I didn't view the pain as suffering from a curse but as a joyful, trusting, willful submission to my loving Creator's design. I did not feel fear but a peace that passes understanding (Phil 4:7). I felt loved and cherished by God and those around me.

Unfortunately I could find no Christian books to help me embrace the beauty of childbirth and God's transformation of my heart in the process. I had to turn to New Age birthing books that gave sound labor advice but also spoke of "the goddess within." My third birth convinced me that most Christians are not thinking biblically about childbirth and that we do so to our own detriment. Jesus' followers should be the ones proclaiming peace and God's presence, rather than fear.

The "Right" Kind of Birth

Many women who opt for an unmedicated childbirth do so to avoid the potential side effects of pain medications or to prove to themselves or others that they can. Some also recognize the sacredness of childbirth and seek understanding through natural labor and delivery. These women are often scoffed at for supposedly displaying machismo, enduring needless pain and suffering though pain relief medication is available. These women recognize something about birth that is often overlooked: The process of childbirth transforms us.

When we view labor only through the lens of pain and fear, we *will* experience severe pain and find reasons to fear. Our expectations for labor and delivery affect our experience of it. As Christians we have access to the Prince of Peace; why do we not expect or ask for peace during childbirth? Our anxiety obscures our view of our caring Creator as we deliver new life into the world, and it masks

God's immeasurable love for mothers as they participate in the miracle he performs.

As a childbirth educator and doula, I have an obvious bias toward unmedicated childbirth free of unnecessary interventions, because I strongly believe (and studies prove) that for low-risk, healthy mothers and babies, this is generally safest. It is also in its natural form that we can see God's design in childbirth most clearly. However, this does not invalidate the birth experiences of mothers who have had cesarean sections or pain medication, whether by necessity or by choice. These births can still be fully satisfying, transformative, and worshipful experiences.

There is a tendency among women who opt for unmedicated labor to view women who choose pain medication as weak, and for women who choose pain medication to view women who want unmedicated labors as "macho." Such attitudes reveal unkind, insensitive, and proud hearts. My purpose in this book is not to hold up one way as best. Instead, I encourage women to think deeply about the way God designed women's bodies to handle the stresses and struggle of childbirth and what he intended by doing so. And if things go wrong, we should remember that the process is tinged with the effects of sin and point to our great need for Someone to redeem creation. Indeed, we should thank God for modern medical marvels that save the lives of women and babies and for medicines that bring relief during a long struggle. This book does not pass judgment on those with various birth experiences and wishes and pain tolerances—or worse, tack on the descriptor of "biblical" to one particular type of birth. I'm not concerned with the details of the birth as much as whether a mother has a spiritual perspective on her labor and delivery and can see how Christ is in it all.

I am less concerned about what kind of birth a mother chooses—unmedicated, medicated, elective cesarean—as long as *she* makes these choices as the primary active participant in her birth. Our birthing experiences are unique, reflecting our many different needs, personalities, fears, and hopes. For most women who give birth throughout the world, childbirth choices are made for them by others or by routine procedures that are not to be questioned, though they may do more harm than good. Women are often violated, stripped of their dignity, and made to feel out of control of their own bodies during a time that should be powerful and transformative. Sometimes emergencies happen or medical intervention is necessary, but caregivers must hear an expectant mother's input, perspective, and consent so these decisions can be made *with* the mother. This way, even a difficult birth does not have to be a trauma done to her but a difficult road she walked with dignity and with concerned helpers beside her. Women and their caregivers should be allies, not enemies battling for control.

Childbirth is not primarily a medical event; it is a major chapter in a woman's story. It is a chapter she will retell over and over throughout her life. While I advocate for changes that restore dignity to birth, women are not doomed to be victims of the healthcare system. We make choices—such as whether to educate ourselves or to take medication without asking questions, to find a caregiver who listens to us or to continue seeing a doctor we don't like—and we bear responsibility for those choices.

Our caregivers will fade from our story; they are not responsible for bringing meaning and satisfaction to our birth. As mothers, we need to be sure we are making good birth choices for our babies and ourselves. When we understand that childbirth is a holy process, we should want to treat it as a sacred turn in our stories. A proper theology of childbirth leads us to seek justice, safety, and dignity in obstetric care for women globally.

The Gospel and Childbirth

The Bible often doesn't give the specific tips and tricks we desperately seek for our daily lives as parents. The Bible doesn't tell us whether the Bradley Method or Lamaze is better, whether we should or shouldn't use pacifiers, where the baby should sleep and in what position, or whether we should potty-train at age two, three, or four.[2] The Bible doesn't give advice about how to have a better childbirth experience. We can certainly ask God for wisdom, which he gives generously (Jas 1:5). We can look to the wisdom of experienced mothers in our local church. But there is a lot of freedom regarding childbirth and parenting methods, because the Bible doesn't specifically address them. The Bible is not ultimately about these decisions, so we need to take care not to elevate their importance more highly than they deserve.

Instead, the Bible is about God, who created us and loved us, who grieved as we sinned and separated ourselves from him, and who sent his Son to reconcile us to himself. Those brought into God's family are sealed with God's own Spirit and have full and free access to God (Eph 4:30; 2:18). This relates to childbirth and parenting because Jesus is the "wisdom from God," available to us when we ask (1 Cor 1:30). God is changing our hearts to be conformed into his image more and more as we move through life toward and with him (Rom 8:29).

When we put childbirth in a biblical perspective, within the context of the gospel, it becomes clearer for us. We encounter God as we ask him for wisdom for our childbirth choices, for grace in labor, and patience in the last long weeks of pregnancy. We come to him and repent, confessing our pride or lack of trust. Regardless of birth choices or outcomes we find grace and not shame in Christ, who nailed our shame to the cross (Col 2:14). When we press into Jesus, our wounds are bound up and our traumas are healed. As we approach labor we lay aside guilt, fear, and insecurities about our choices and what others might think. We rest in Christ, knowing that he loves us and is pleased with us. In childbirth, one of the most common experiences among women, we find the gospel proclaimed and grace lavished on us by God.

A Glimpse of God's Purposes in Childbirth

This book explores the theme of childbirth in the Bible, what childbirth teaches us about God, and how God uses the experience to shape the souls of the women giving birth. Childbirth is complicated, unpredictable, emotional, spiritual, and deeply physical. Our experiences with childbirth are as varied as we are! How could one book possibly honor every childbirth experience, comfort every hurt, and speak the gospel into every situation? How can we see childbirth from every perspective and accurately portray childbirth and God's work in it for every woman?

The truth is, we can't. "For now we see through a glass, darkly" (1 Cor 13:12 KJV), but in this book we will catch at least a glimpse of what God is doing through this important event.

As you process your past childbirth experience or experience to come, I pray that you will lean into Jesus and that you will see him more clearly through childbirth—whatever that may look like for you. While the Bible doesn't contain proof texts for how to have an ideal birth, I hope you see the gospel illuminated through childbirth.

In chapter 1, we will revisit Eve's sin in Genesis 3—a passage long used to denigrate the birth experience as a curse and deny women pain relief in labor so they receive the full blow of God's judgment against women. We will find that Eve is not actually cursed (it's true!) and that God does not carry out his anger on women in childbirth, but uses childbirth for restoration and redemption. We also will explore Paul's confusing statement in 1 Timothy that women are "saved through childbearing" (2:15).

Chapter 2 explores the ways women reflect Yahweh through childbirth as they cocreate with him, suffer and long for their children as God longs for his people, and nurse their children as God nourishes and provides for his.

Chapter 3 considers the profound idea that God himself participated in childbirth as a baby. We will see how the incarnation imparts sacredness and dignity to childbirth and what women can learn from Mary as she carried and delivered the Son of God.

Chapter 4 discusses the biblical metaphor of childbirth as entry into the kingdom of God and conversion as a rebirth through the Holy Spirit. In light of this coming kingdom and our role as agents who advance it, we will also uncover how dangerous and unjust birth practices can be improved in accordance with God's coming reign.

Chapter 5 explores childbirth as a biblical metaphor for suffering and overcoming. We find childbirth as preparation for and a representation of suffering in other areas of life as we model Jesus' suffering in love for another—not as self-pitying martyrs but as strong women of valor. We see childbirth as a physical picture of the biblical theme of pain, suffering, and resurrection.

Finally, chapter 6 delves into the God's providence in opening and closing wombs, the problem of infertility in the Bible and in our lives, and his intimate work in creating new life.

Laboring with Christ

After each of the six chapters is a section called "Laboring with Christ," which offers spiritually formative practices and exercises for seeking Christ through pregnancy and childbirth. This section may be especially practical for pregnant women to use alongside their prenatal education classes as they prepare not only their bodies and minds but also their hearts and souls for childbirth. These spiritual disciplines or practices require effort both in action steps and in retraining our minds as we consider how Jesus transforms our whole selves, not just our bodies or our souls (as if they were independent of each another).

Many people treat spiritual disciplines as practices used to earn God's approval, so we need to talk about this very carefully. If you are praying, fasting, or reading your Bible so that you will get brownie points with God or get him to like you more, you need to remind yourself of the gospel: "While we were still sinners, Christ died for us" (Rom 5:8). While you were still a total wreck, bent over in shame, or a self-righteous person who outwardly did every-thing correctly, Christ died for you and offered you grace simply because of his great mercy and love. God freely offered his mercy to his worst enemies on the planet to the glory of his grace: to the idol-worshiping and forgetful and disobedient Israelites, to the barbaric people of Nineveh, to those who shouted, "Crucify him!" and to the zealous terrorist Saul. We do nothing to earn God's mercy; how could we possibly?

Salvation is by the grace of God through faith, not by works (Eph 2:8-9). Grace is infused even into our discipleship. God himself is conforming us to the image of his Son; this cannot be achieved simply by trying harder. But we play an active role in our spiritual formation. We bring ourselves to God through various spiritual disciplines—such as prayer, fasting, studying Scripture, and lamenting—and he works in us in ways we could never take credit for.

This is the idea behind the spiritual disciplines in these sections: not earning God's love but *laying hold* of God's love intentionally. Spiritual training is not strenuous work we complete with our own effort, as if we could try hard enough to be holy and succeed. It also isn't something left entirely up to God, as if we were passive recipients of a sneak attack of the fruits of the Spirit. We labor with God for our discipleship (Phil 2:12–13). These exercises will not make you instantly holy, but they can enable the process of opening up your life to God, who changes you.

Childbirth brings us to God in a very unique way: in wonder and awe, in fear and sometimes agony, in loss of control and anchoring ourselves to him. It can be traumatic, transformative, painless, agonizing, anxious, beautiful, and messy. Childbirth is complex and unpredictable. And God uses it as grace in our lives to make us more like him. Spiritual disciplines are ways of opening up our hearts and focusing our attention on God's work in us so that we don't miss it. Spiritual disciplines help us to live awake and alert to God, and they drive us toward him in worship.

Spiritual disciplines are not designed to turn us into hermits; many of them are done in the context of the community of the church. This allows us to pray for, encourage, teach, forgive, and challenge one another, and it also prevents us from thinking we are holier than we really are. People shine light on our faults and bring us opportunities for repentance and sanctification. The church might consider the ways it can help in the spiritual training of its childbearing members, as well as learn from them, so that we might be together affirmed in Christ.

It can be tempting to put off learning new disciplines in the sleep-deprived, hectic days of pregnancy, newborns, and toddlers, reasoning that when our children grow older, things will become easier. Consider making your devotional life even more disciplined during this time precisely *because* of the craziness of this season. These years are deeply formative for moms, perhaps because of their intensity. Holding God's merciful grace before you at all times, press into him so that you can be transformed by him into the godly mother you need to be.

I also don't intend for you to practice every exercise listed at the end of each chapter. Sometimes when we see a long list, we either become overwhelmed or turn it into a legalistic pursuit. The point is engaging with God and allowing him to work in us. If that means choosing one exercise out of the entire book and doing it again and again for a year, that's great! If that means incorporating many disciplines, or revising disciplines you already practice to put childbirth into a biblical perspective, that's also great.

Pregnancy and childbirth are also significant for the father as he supports his wife and learns self-denial more intensely. Many men find that witnessing their wives give birth changes them in ways difficult to articulate. Childbirth shapes men, too. However, it is beyond the scope of this book—as well as beyond my experience and expertise—to explore how childbirth shapes the souls of men. Please, dads, don't feel that I've intentionally left you out. My focus here is on the mother, who undergoes more obvious change in many ways.

As I studied the Bible's imagery of childbirth and how God himself participates in this process, I found myself on my face, weeping in awe of God, over and over. This book began about birth and ended as a book about worship, through the very common female experience of childbirth. As we see God and encounter him through his Son—even in childbirth—we are transformed. Join me as we find God in the metaphors and realities of childbearing and allow him to bear fruit in us.

CHAPTER 1

Eve's Curse and Our Narrative of God

When the Spirit has changed our narratives [about God] sufficiently, we begin to think differently. As a result we begin to believe in and trust a good and loving God who is strong and powerful.

—James K. A. Smith, *The Good and Beautiful God*[1]

All Eve's Fault

After a busy day of scrubbing baseboards, organizing freshly laundered baby clothes, and rearranging our apartment to make way for a makeshift nursery, I settled into the recliner at 10 p.m. The nesting instinct had hit me all in one day, and my urge to clean and organize made no concessions for my very pregnant state. I breathed through an uncomfortable contraction and consulted Google for the 10th time on early signs of labor. I concluded this was probably just another Braxton-Hicks contraction, preparing my uterus for labor. Suddenly a searing pain shot up through my bottom, and I slid out of my chair onto the floor, anxiously contorting my body. When it passed, I assumed I had exerted myself too much that day and joined my husband in bed.

Two hours later I awoke to more contractions with the same knifelike feeling. (I later learned that this sensation was my cervix dilating.) The waves were coming every seven to nine minutes; I was in labor! My husband and I rushed to the hospital, worried that I would give birth in the car, as we'd seen in far too many movies. As I worked through each contraction, I focused all of my birth rage not on my husband (to his relief) but on Eve: "You just *had* to eat that stupid fruit!"

The "Curse" of Eve

It's no secret that childbirth is painful. Egyptian women used opium, the basis of morphine, to ease labor pains. The women of the Andes chewed coca leaves, from which we get cocaine. In the West, obstetricians have experimented with chloroform, ether, narcotics, tranquilizers, and laughing gas. One horrific method called twilight sleep didn't reduce pain, but it did erase mothers' memories of the entire birth. Today the pain relief of choice in the United States is the epidural, in which an anesthetic shot between vertebrae numbs the mother's lower body while allowing her to remain lucid during the birth.

For Christian women, however, pain relief during labor has not always been allowed. Citing the "curse of Eve" in Genesis 3, religious authorities denied pain relief to laboring mothers, reasoning that women would be evading God's judgment upon them. Painful labor is what women deserve, and painful labor is what they shall get, or so the thinking goes. In 1591, Euphemia Maclean requested pain relief—a potion including body parts from a corpse—as she labored with her twins. King James VI condemned her to be burned at the stake, and her midwife was executed for witchcraft.[2] The much less extreme (and likely more effective) pain relievers chloroform and ether were condemned as a "decoy of Satan" by clerics in the 19th century.[3] Even today, some Christians believe that for God to be pleased, laboring moms should refuse epidurals and other forms of pain relief. Secular books on birth almost universally poke fun at the Bible's "curse of Eve," claiming

Christianity denigrates women and denies them the choice and dignity they deserve.

John Dye, an obstetrician working in the late 1800s through early 1900s, noted the irony that though many Christians opposed pain relief due to the supposed curse of childbirth, they didn't hesitate to seek pain relief for themselves from other ailments resulting from the fall. An advocate of better obstetric practices that would provide women with natural pain relief in labor, Dye concluded, "For our part we cannot believe the Almighty the cruel, merciless tyrant many picture Him, but believe in His wisdom, mercy and justice. He has placed at our disposal abundant means for our relief if we will but comprehend and apply them."[4]

Some cite Eve's curse as proof that the Bible is a myth, for many women have experienced painless or nearly painless births. The Discovery Life Channel show *I Didn't Know I Was Pregnant* tells stories of women who went through their entire pregnancies unaware they had conceived. They often thought they needed to go to the bathroom or perhaps had cramps from the stomach flu, and they ended up delivering newborns while relaxing in the bathtub or straining on the toilet. In many cases, they never felt enough labor pain to consider going to the hospital. The first half of *Ina May's Guide to Childbirth* is a compilation of positive birth stories. While many women did experience pain and struggle through birth, some speak of completely painless birth, and some even experienced an orgasm during the pushing phase.[5] Most of these women describe their childbirth experiences as formative, spiritual, and healing—not in terms of being cursed, in pain, or afraid.

Reading through stories of painless or ecstatic births led me to a crisis with Genesis 3. My own first birth experience seemed to confirm the curse, but how can women be universally cursed with pain if some experience painless or even orgasmic births? Is painful labor truly God's judgment on all women for the sin of Eve? And if secular and New Age women experience peace, transformation, and love in childbirth, then why is that not a common experience for women indwelled by the Holy Spirit and joined to Christ? Does childbirth truly have to be a painful, cursed experience?

A Second Look at Genesis 3

Tradition holds that Moses wrote the book of Genesis for the nation of Israel as they made their way to the promised land after the exodus. While most Western Christians scour the first chapters of Genesis looking for the age of the earth or an argument against Darwinism, Genesis would have answered much more straightforward questions for its original audience, like, "Who is Yahweh?" In the beginning, Yahweh—not Baal, Rah, or any of the pagan gods their neighbors worshiped—created the heavens and the earth. He subdued the chaos of the waters, created the heavens, brought forth land, and filled the earth with all kinds of creatures. It was good.

Then God formed man from the dust and breathed life into him. God planted a garden called Eden and put the man in it to cultivate and take care of it. Yahweh had grown two trees in the middle: the tree of life and the tree of the knowledge of good and evil. God told Adam, "You are free to eat from any tree in the garden; but you must not eat from the tree of the knowledge of good and evil, for when you eat from it you will certainly die" (Gen 2:16–17). As God had named Adam, so Adam named the livestock, birds, and wild animals; but no helper was found for Adam. Yahweh put Adam in a deep sleep, took a rib, and formed from it a woman. Adam called her "woman," for she was taken from the man. God blessed them and commanded them to multiply.

In Eden all was as it should be: Humans walked with God and in harmony with each other, blessed by God to multiply and to cultivate an already-planted garden. Most of all, they had Yahweh's presence—there was no shame in their nakedness with each other or before God, and it was all "very good" (1:31). The Hebrew word for this goodness and harmony is *shalom*—"universal flourishing, wholeness, and delight."[6]

The Israelites listened to this Genesis story from the wilderness, between Egypt and the promised land. Their entire existence revolved around Yahweh's presence among them. They saw his plagues trump the gods of Egypt, heard his thunderous voice on

Sinai, followed his pillars of fire and cloud, and constructed the tabernacle—a portable precursor to the temple—where the holy of holies resided. God's frequent promise to Israel was that he would be their God and they would be his people, and he would be with them. God's presence among Israel was of primary concern.

When we approach Genesis 3, we often read it only through Paul's eyes as the story where "sin entered the world through one man, and death through sin" (Rom 5:12). Of course, this reading is not wrong. A solid understanding of when our sin nature arose and how it affects us today is important for understanding the gospel. But the question that drives Genesis 3 for the original audience of Israelites would have been this: "How did Israel get cast out of God's divine presence?" John Walton puts it well: "In Israel, while there was undoubtedly a recognition of the inherent nature of sin, the biggest problem of the Fall was not concentrated in the change in human nature or the heart condition but in the loss of access to the presence of God and the reduced ability to participate in the blessing. ... Throughout all the rest of the Old Testament one never hears talk of regaining the comfort of Eden, but regaining access to God's presence was paramount."[7]

The *shalom* scene of creation closes, and the next act begins in Genesis 3. The crafty serpent questioned the woman about God's goodness and fairness: "Did God really say, 'You must not eat from *any* tree in the garden'?" (3:1). The woman corrected the serpent, saying that no, just the tree in the middle of the garden was forbidden—though she curiously added that God had said not even to touch it, which was not true (3:3). Perhaps this is a small sign that Eve's trust in Yahweh's goodness to her was weakening. Now the serpent lied. "You will *not* certainly die," he says (3:4). The serpent tricked Eve into eating the fruit by telling her that she could be like God, knowing good and evil. She gave the fruit to Adam, who remained mysteriously silent through the entire conversation, and he ate. Their eyes were opened, and they knew they were naked. In their shame, they fashioned coverings from fig leaves. Then they heard Yahweh walking in the garden, and they hid.

The Hebrew word used here for Yahweh's walking sounds implies habitual walking, suggesting God often walked through Eden in the cool of the day.[8] Yahweh and the humans would normally have fellowship during these walks, but Adam and Eve were hiding in futility behind trees from the creator and sustainer of the universe. The relationship with him they once had, the *shalom*, had been broken. Life was no longer as it should be.

At the time of this writing, my older children are four and two, and it strikes me as somewhat comical that they often have the same shameful reaction as Adam and Eve when they have disobeyed me. I am not omniscient, but they are bad hiders and I know all their hiding places. A normal day with my children is filled with, "Mama, look at this! Mama, do you see me? Mama, I want that! Mama! Mama!" I know when they have disobeyed because our noisy space suddenly becomes quiet, and when I check on them, they are hiding with the aftermath of whatever disaster they have caused. It is always easy to find them, but the relational distance is harder to overcome. They sense they cannot come to me in their shame. They cannot ask for what they need or play with me while this mess lies between us. Where can Adam and Eve hide from Yahweh? What has this sin done to their relationship that they *hide* instead of walk with him in the cool of the day?

God called to Adam, drawing them out gently, saying, "Where are you?" (3:9). Adam, avoiding the real issue, responded that he hid when he heard God in the garden, because he was naked. Yahweh asked who told him he was naked, but he didn't wait for the answer before launching his interrogation. "Have you eaten from the tree that I commanded you not to eat from?" (3:11). Adam justified himself and shifted the blame to "the woman you put here with me" (3:12). Adam now considered the woman, God's gift to Adam as a companion and helper, a mistake. God, the giver of life and good gifts, was to blame for creating her.

The woman did some blame shifting of her own when she was questioned: "The serpent deceived me" (3:13). There was no relationship to be maintained or redeemed—God did not interrogate the serpent but immediately cursed it:

Because you have done this,

Cursed are you above all livestock
  and all wild animals!
You will crawl on your belly
  and you will eat dust
  all the days of your life.
And I will put enmity
  between you and the woman,
  and between your offspring and hers;
he will crush your head,
  and you will strike his heel (Gen 3:14–15).

First, God gave the reason for the cursing: "because *you* have done this." The serpent, it is important to note, is the *only* one of the three to be cursed in this passage (along with the ground). A curse, rather than just a hex for bad luck, removes someone from God's protection, favor, and presence.[9] This passage isn't etiological—that is, its purpose is not to explain why snakes don't have legs. Crawling on the belly and eating dust are terms of *humiliation*, not biology. The serpent is a representation of evil, death, and sin,[10] and God marked out its future: It will not win.

God had words only of condemnation for the serpent, but his words to the couple maintained some hope, a hint that the blessing was not lost for them.[11] The serpent tricked the woman and was responsible in many ways for her downfall; his offspring will be at war with hers, and one of her offspring will eventually gain the upper hand. In the Hebrew, "crush" and "strike" are the same word, so the New International Version's translation of them as remarkably nuanced words is based on church history's interpretation of the passage rather than an accurate reflection of the text. Still, a strike against a heel and a strike against the head are not equal blows. The passage likely implies the victory of the woman's offspring—Jesus. Genesis 3:15 is sometimes called the *protevangelium*, the "first gospel."

To the woman [God] said,

"I will make your pains [*itsavon*] in childbearing very severe;
    with painful labor [*etsev*] you will give birth to children.
Your desire will be for your husband,
    and he will rule over you" (Gen 3:16).

The first two lines contain the English words "pains" and "painful," and as our cultural experience and expectation of childbirth focuses solely on *physical* pain, we assume this is where pain in childbirth originated. The word translated as "pains" is the Hebrew word *itsavon*. In this form, this word is found in only two other places in the Bible, Genesis 3:17 and 5:29—both translated as "painful toil," and in connection with the cursed ground not giving up food easily. Why is this word translated as "pains" here, but when used for Adam just one verse later, it is translated as "painful toil"? Nouns that derive from this word are most often used to express not only *physical* pain but also agony, grief, and anguish.[12] The word *atsav*, found in *itsavon,* also occurs in Genesis 6:6, where God saw the evil of the people he created and was "deeply troubled" (*atsav*) in his heart. Many older English translations render the word "sorrow" rather than pain. Perhaps our negative view of childbirth led English translators to choose the word "pain" when "toil" or "anguish" would be a better fit. Physical pain isn't excluded from this word, but childbirth is more than a physical event; it is an experience that engages a woman's mind, body, and emotions in a way that few other experiences do.

To some, this may seem like bickering over similar words. Whether you render it "pain" or "anguish," childbirth still comes out in a negative light. But language is important, and it shapes the way we experience things. If women expect, from this passage, inescapably severe physical pain in childbirth as judgment from God, their expectations will likely be met as they labor and fight against cursed bodies. "Sorrow" or even "toil," however, have different connotations—they encompass the emotional aspects of childbearing. Perhaps Genesis tells us something about childbirth other than that it is physically painful for women.

Many childbirth educators teach that pain is inextricably tied to fear in the mother in childbirth, and so they teach relaxation techniques to overcome these fears to reduce pain. Grantly Dick-Read's classic book *Childbirth Without Fear* is based on the principle that overcoming fear can help a mother eliminate the majority—or even all—of her pain in childbirth. In his book, he recounts the incredible story of a woman who was in labor and about to push her baby out. When he brought her a chloroform mask, she refused it and calmly gave birth to her baby. When he asked her why she had refused the chloroform, she said, "It didn't hurt. It wasn't meant to, was it, doctor?"[13] His famous description of the "fear-tension-pain" cycle forms the basis of many prenatal classes: Fear of childbirth causes a woman's body to tense up and resist childbirth, which causes increased pain—which causes even more fear. Midwife Ina May Gaskin writes that fear and anxiety can cause the cervix to stop dilating or even close back up, extending labor for hours or even days, as she has seen with many of her patients.[14]

The mind-body connection is often underestimated. If physical pain in childbirth can be greatly reduced or even overcome by better birth positions, education, and a peaceful mental state, then perhaps Genesis 3 speaks of another sort of anguish. If the curse of pain in childbirth doesn't carry over to all women and all cultures, then we have reason to doubt our presuppositions about Genesis 3. Pain may be part of this equation, but it isn't the full idea.

The word translated in Genesis 3:16 as "childbearing" in most English Bibles is unmistakably "conception," but as conception itself is not painful, the translators changed this to "childbearing" to make it match the word "pain."[15] Thus, God's first line to the woman is not about an increased pain in childbirth but rather an increased anxiety over conception. The "painful labor" (*etsev*) in the second line indicates the strenuous work of giving birth. The two lines are joined by a figure of speech called hendiadys, which joins two nouns with "and," giving the idea that they are two parts of the same idea (an English example is "nice and warm"). Together, the two lines encompass the entire process of conception through childbirth. Hence, a better rendering might be, "I will increase your anguish in conception and childbirth, and with strenuous labor you will give birth to children."

When we assume that because of Eve's sin God has *cursed* all women with pain in childbirth—the worst kind of pain, we are told—what does that tell us about the way we view God? That he is unleashing his wrath upon women each time they give birth? We do not have this same presupposition about men who labor in the fields. They labor with difficulty on a ground that God cursed, but their work is not considered useless, cursed, and painful. God *did not* curse the woman; he desires to maintain a relationship with her and redeem her, unlike with the serpent. He loves her. But the consequence of her sin was given before she talked to the serpent: God had said if they ate the fruit from that tree, *they would certainly die* (Gen 2:17).

Death is now part of the world, and childbearing, from conception to birth to parenting, is an event with legitimate fears because it is tinged with death. We see in this story that sin ushers into the world guilt, shame, and fear—before God and between the humans. Women who are trying to conceive or who are pregnant are almost always fearful. *Will I be able to get pregnant? Will I miscarry? Will the baby be healthy? Will I be able to handle childbirth? Will I die in childbirth? Will I outlive my children?* There is sorrow and worry from conception to birth and beyond because death is now part of the system. The blessing "be fruitful and increase in number" (Gen 1:28), while still a blessing, is now laced with danger and death. The weight of the broken *shalom* in Eden is heavy, because the wages of sin is death. Miscarriage, stillbirth, toxemia, hemorrhage, obstructed births, and many other threats to the life of the mother and child are heartbreaking realities in this world after that first sin. Our anguish has indeed been increased. But it is not cursed.

Finally, God described Adam's punishment:

> Because you listened to your wife and ate fruit from the
> tree about which I commanded you, "You must not eat
> from it,"

> Cursed is the ground because of you;
>> through painful toil you will eat food from it
>> all the days of your life.
> It will produce thorns and thistles for you,
>> and you will eat the plants of the field.
> By the sweat of your brow
>> you will eat your food
> until you return to the ground,
>> since from it you were taken;
> for dust you are
>> and to dust you will return (Gen 3:17–19).

God begins by holding Adam accountable for what he has done. No more blame shifting. God curses the ground "because of" Adam, and while the blessing of seed-bearing plants to eat remains, the blessing is now tinged with death: Adam will have to work hard to produce food, and much of his work will be wasted as the ground produces thistles and thorns. Adam's anguish comes from the curse of the ground. While modern industrialized and commercialized food production often disconnects us from this reality, the unyielding ground is still a hardship for farmers and agrarian societies around the world. Bad soil, pollution runoff, droughts, floods, and pests and parasites can wipe out an entire crop. Farmers are left with little to show for a season of hard work. Many people in this world suffer from poverty and malnutrition because of the cursed ground.[16]

God warned that eating the fruit would cause death, so Adam will return to the dust from which he was formed. It is interesting that just after Genesis 3:19, which is heavy on death, verse 20 seemingly out of nowhere says that Adam named his wife Eve, "mother of all the living." Perhaps the author reminds us of hope even in the death sentence: The blessing of procreation remains, and through this blessing will come the triumph of her offspring over evil. The death sentence for the couple was passed when God exiled them from Eden, thereby banishing them from access to the tree of life.

But before Adam and Eve left the garden, God's grace was given in the form of skins for clothing. Clothing in the ancient world was a universal symbol of a person's rank and role in society. Nakedness was shame; being clothed by someone honorable raised up those in shame—a frequent theme throughout the Bible. Replacing their scarcely functional fig leaves, God clothed them in an unexpectedly merciful gesture. He gave them unmerited honor to replace their shame. He gave them grace even as they were exiled from Eden, hinting at the redemption to come. One day, humanity will be clothed with honor and immortality in Christ that will cover their nakedness and shame (2 Cor 5:2–5).

We must understand God's heart as we seek understanding concerning childbirth in Genesis 3. Even in Eve's sorrow, we see hope. We see God's love and caring provision for her and her husband. In cursing the serpent, God promises that the woman's offspring—though born in anguish—will bring victory. Eve is not doomed, and the blessing is not removed. As a child bearer, she will play a critical role in freeing humanity from the consequences of sin as she becomes "mother of all the living" and, eventually, as the Messiah is born through her line (Luke 3:38).[17] The blessing and the punishment are now interwoven: She will bring forth the offspring in suffering, but he will ultimately crush her enemy. The woman's anguish in childbearing is both a reminder of that first sin and the vehicle of her salvation from sin. And it can serve as a reminder for women as we labor too. The Deliverer is coming back to wipe away every tear, crush the serpent's head, and bring death to death.

Saved through Childbearing?

Understanding Eve's role in salvation as a child bearer can help us comprehend Paul's confusing words to Timothy: "But women will be saved through childbearing—if they continue in faith, love and holiness with propriety" (1 Tim 2:15). The potential misinterpretation of this passage is distressing. If we do not reconcile this passage with the rest of Paul's teachings on salvation, we might believe that women are subject to salvation through works, contingent upon their ability to bear children. We should be alarmed about such an interpretation! Paul's anthem throughout his other letters is salvation by God's grace through faith—not works. Some have proposed that this passage teaches that godly women will be *physically* saved through childbirth. But while the semantic range for the Greek verb used for "saved" includes physical rescue, history is full of many godly women who have died in childbirth. How, then, should we read this verse?

Paul's statement occurs in the context of an argument he gives against the Ephesian Christian women behaving as the "new Roman woman"—who dressed both ostentatiously and provocatively and who derided wifehood and motherhood in favor of a sexual revolution.[18] These wealthy Ephesian women embraced a heresy that forbade marriage and childbearing (1 Tim 4:3), and they even advocated abortion.[19] The main concern of Paul's letter to Timothy is missiological—how can the church in Ephesus reflect Christ to their neighbors? Paul's instructions to the church throughout the letter are focused on their public image by good deeds and holiness. Paul was concerned that Christian women were imitating the new Roman woman and shunning God's good gift of marriage and procreation—thus, promoting this heresy.

The social norm for women at this time was marriage, which usually resulted in children. Paul is not setting up a command condemning childless women; he is pointing women away from a heresy and toward a godly domestic life. This passage is often used today in the church to argue that a "good Christian woman" should be a quiet, submissive, stay-at-home mom and wife. The difference between our cultural norms and that of first-century Ephesus are vast. In Western society today, women—at least in theory—are generally viewed as equals to men. They have educational opportunities, are considered valid witnesses in court, hold teaching positions, are not arranged in marriage, and are able to remain single and/or childless without raising concerns about promoting heresy. By saying women are "saved through childbearing," Paul is essentially saying, "It is a lie that women should not marry or have children, and you have been deceived as Eve was deceived."

John Stott argues that this passage is best interpreted as "women will be saved through The Childbirth," that is, the birth of Christ.[20] Since Paul quotes Genesis 2–3 in the immediate context, where redemption is foretold to come through the offspring of the woman, this argument is a good possibility. Paul normally speaks about salvation in terms of Christ's death and resurrection rather than his birth. However, in this passage the connection of women to salvation is in birth: Eve's childbearing led to the offspring, who would crush the head of the serpent. Mary participated in this prophecy by giving birth to the Messiah, who brought salvation. Women are saved through faith in Jesus, not through their childbearing abilities. A heresy that denigrates the method that the Savior entered the world—childbirth—should certainly be set right.

Peace for the Christian Mother

In general, childbirth usually *does* hurt. It's difficult for an eight-pound (give or take) baby to emerge from a small opening in a sensitive area of the body. But it is also true that our fears and expectations of pain, as well as modern attitudes and practices for childbirth, actually *increase* our pain. I was never so fearful of childbirth as I was with my firstborn, when I believed that women were cursed with pain in childbirth, and it proved to be the most painful experience of my life. It was a self-fulfilling prophecy. After a few hours of my first contractions, I lay on the bed and cried—not from pain, as labor was not yet difficult, but from fear of what the next hours held. I tensed all my muscles, straining against each contraction. At the hospital, I was taken to the labor ward in a wheelchair, which seemed to confirm the danger of the coming hours. The nurses hooked me up to an IV, assessed my pain levels on a scale of 1 to 10, and offered me pain relief. It seemed liked a medical event.

My doctor came in, ordered Pitocin against my wishes to speed things up, and accidentally overdosed me. The contractions came so hard and fast that I hyperventilated, unable to stay on top of the pain. A nurse yelled at me to stop, saying that I was hurting my baby by depriving him of oxygen. My husband, normally everyone's best friend, pushed her out of my face and told her to stop yelling at me. I felt sure that something was very wrong and wondered if my baby and I would survive this. I apologized in gasps to everyone in the room—for not suffering stoically, for hurting my baby, for being a failure as a woman. I was sure that I was dying. As I pushed in the last minutes of my agony, my doctor rushed in and barked at me to stop pushing so he could put his boots on over his shoes. I took a deep breath, made a wish to ruin his expensive shoes to repay him for the Pitocin, and pushed harder than ever. The doctor barely caught Breckon, and I received a large tear for my disobedience. When I sat up an hour later, I saw all the blood—I had hemorrhaged.

In talking to many women over the years about their childbirth experiences, I have heard my story echo in theirs. The expectations of horrific pain, the increase of pain and fear by hospital protocols, the distress caused by medical staff who ignore and belittle and even yell at laboring mothers—these make childbearing unbearable. If we believe that childbirth should be a curse, that laboring women should suffer extreme pain and be stripped of dignity because of Eve's sin, then we will continue to allow these practices that hurt mothers and perhaps even consider them normal. But if we embrace a new narrative—the gospel embedded even in the early chapters of Genesis—then we will follow a God who loves women and gave his own Son to restore women to *shalom*. We will seek peace for mothers in labor. We will seek a laboring woman's dignity and help her see Jesus in the delivery room. We will stop treating mothers as mere wombs but as whole persons.

My third birth occurred at a freestanding birth center, attended by two midwives and my husband. During my appointments, after the midwives checked my vitals, they asked about my fears, my hopes for my birth, and whether I had any concerns. When I went into labor early one morning, I sent my husband to drop off the boys with friends. While alone, I rocked back and forth with my hands on my belly, praying that the Lord would deliver my daughter safely and that he would be near to me in the next hours. I relaxed. I sensed sacredness in these moments of bringing a new soul into the world, feeling that God himself took joy in it. By late morning, my contractions were slowing down rather than speeding up, so my husband and I went for a walk to encourage the baby to move down. We came in when I got tired, and I timed my contractions. They had gone from 5 minutes apart to 12 minutes—the wrong way! As I was resting and wondering if we had dropped off our sons too soon, a powerful contraction came and my water broke. The waves became much more intense and regular, but still not something I would describe as painful, only powerful. We drove to the birth center, as I tend to dilate quickly once in active labor.

Through each contraction, I focused on relaxing my muscles rather than fighting through the contractions and bracing myself, as I naturally wanted to do. It felt like surrendering to something good rather than fighting a curse. When a contraction would start and I fought it, it hurt. As soon as I relaxed my muscles and focused on breathing deeply, the pain subsided. Relaxing and breathing deeply was hard, focused, intense work. Smiling midwives greeted me at the birth center in a comfortable, dimly lit room, with candles lit and soft music playing. I instantly felt peace and calm. This wasn't an emergency; it was a happy day! The midwife drew a warm bath, and I settled into it just as a contraction was coming. The warm water eased my muscles even more, and each contraction was much easier to manage. Between waves, I joked and laughed with my husband and felt a sense of awe, joy, and peace.

After only five minutes in the tub I felt an urge to push, and my midwife noticed it too. I asked her if I was allowed to push—I wasn't in enough pain to be so close to the end! She laughed, saying, "Trust your body and just let it do what it needs to do." I reminded myself that God had created my body and the childbirth process and that I could trust him as I labored. The next contraction brought more serious pushing. I experienced only about 30 seconds of intense pain and wondered whether I could do it—just as my daughter's head crowned. I let out a deep roar to get her head out through the burning, but as soon as she crowned, the pain subsided. I reached down and touched her head, laughing and exclaiming, "She has so much hair!" Her shoulders were broad and took extra work. My daughter's pink, squishy body slid into her father's hands. She was a full two pounds bigger than her brothers had been, and her birth was nearly painless and completely fearless. She cried just for a few seconds, until she was with me, and then she looked at me with full alertness. I began to cry from joy and adrenaline; I felt energized, even after eight hours of labor—eight hours of hard work, but not eight hours of the "worst pain in the world."

From start to finish, I sensed God's presence with me, his grace to me after two deliveries where I had felt fearful and talked down to by the medical staff. I felt peace and wholeness, as if I was made to do this work, and I felt that God was pleased with me—not because I was birthing in a particular way or place, but because he loves me and I was in a safe environment where I was able to receive it. It was *shalom*. We named our daughter Eden Grace, a reminder of this wholeness and grace given to us by God through her birth.

God's Presence in Childbirth

We may experience anguish during the birthing process, but we are not left alone and hopeless. I believe that for many women, a great deal of this anguish can be eliminated or at least alleviated as a sign of God's presence with us. I believe there are ways we can press into Christ as we seek God's providence over our fertility, as we trust him to carry us while our bodies carry fragile and growing life, and as we experience his love and tender care even during contractions and pushing. We are indwelled by the Holy Spirit. He is with us, and our attentiveness to his presence dispels fear. Understanding God's heart toward women in labor can go a long way in alleviating fear and, thus, pain.

We live between the times. God's presence and healing and restoration have come to us in Christ, but not *fully*, while we live on this side of the new creation. We live in the tension of having access to God's healing, miracles, and presence, but it doesn't mean we live free of the fallout of the fall. In childbirth, as in life, we can experience both his salvation and power as well as the effects of sin. Our bodies sometimes don't act in concert with *shalom*; we miscarry and are sometimes barren, we experience pain and sickness, our babies are sometimes stillborn, and sometimes mothers die giving birth. The anguish of Eve lives on in us as we groan and wait for full redemption of our bodies (Rom 8:22–23).

The Bible begins and ends with the presence of God and *shalom*. The story begins and ends in a garden:

> Then the angel showed me the river of the water of life, as clear as crystal, flowing from the throne of God and of the Lamb down the middle of the great street of the city. On each side of the river stood the tree of life, bearing twelve crops of fruit, yielding its fruit every month. And the leaves of the tree are for the healing of the nations. No longer will there be any curse. The throne of God and of the Lamb will be in the city, and his servants will serve him. They will see his face, and his name will be on their foreheads. There will be no more night. They will not need the light of a lamp or the light of the sun, for the Lord God will give them light. And they will reign for ever and ever (Rev 22:1–5).

The curse is not pain in childbirth; the curse is separation from God, a barrier built by sin and death and exile from Eden. Pain in childbirth, the anguish in whatever form it may come—whether infertility, miscarriage, fear, growing pains, or labor pains—is a reminder of that first sin. This pain recalls our exile from Eden and our departure from *shalom* and God's full presence. Anguish in childbearing reminds us that this is not the way it's supposed to be. This final curtain call from Revelation 22 describes a lush new Eden, with the full restoration of God's presence with his people and complete reconciliation as they bear his name on their foreheads. Even though we may groan during childbirth, we groan in hope, not as abandoned and cursed women. We are loved and redeemed, even as we give birth. I believe it is possible for Christian women to experience this love and peace in God's presence during childbirth.

As we seek God's presence and peace in childbearing, we call out for *shalom*, for life the way God intended. And as we enter the process of childbearing, through pregnancy and birth pangs, through delivery and nursing and nurturing, women reflect the God in whose image they were made. In the next chapter, we will explore Scripture's description of God as a laboring and nursing mother and what childbirth can teach us about the heart of God.

Spiritual Disciplines for Chapter 1

In chapter 1, we learned that childbirth is not about God cursing and punishing women but about his great love, redemption, and restoration. It takes time and intentionality to change our narrative from that of a constantly angry and ready-to-strike God. We must retrain our hearts and minds in the *whole* gospel—that God not only hates sin and its destructiveness, but also gave his own Son's life to restore us so that we no longer hide from him. We must hold side-by-side God's wrath against sin and his love for us.

Israel's primary concern was God's presence among them—a major theme in the early chapters of Genesis. In Christ, we have become the dwelling place of God's presence. But we live in an age of distraction, noise, poor listening, and short attention spans. We need to train ourselves to be attentive to God's presence in our lives, and in childbearing in particular, for with God's presence comes peace and *shalom*.

In this section, we will explore spiritual disciplines that can help us change our false narrative of God, become attentive to his presence, and receive his peace. These exercises are written with the pregnant or laboring mother in mind but can be adapted for anyone. Solitude, meditation, and prayer are typically taught as individual disciplines, but they weave into one another well. These three disciplines clear the space for us to come before God without external distractions so that we may listen and receive from him. This allows us not to separate from the world as hermits but to reengage with the world (or in this case, with labor and delivery) with the mind of Christ.

Solitude

Whether you are introverted or extroverted, solitude can be a challenging discipline. I am an introvert and need time alone to recharge my internal batteries, yet I am often distracted by browsing the internet, texting with friends, or checking things off my to-do lists when I am alone. These aren't bad things—but it isn't true solitude. When we practice solitude, we cut ourselves off from the voices of others in whatever ways they may come, such as physical voices, blogs, books, emails, texts, or phone calls. These people may have good and true things to say, but we need time intentionally listening for the voice of God so we can distinguish truth and goodness.

In solitude we pull away from the need to be approved by others or to seek their justification for our actions or for who we are. We bring ourselves before God, who knows our goodness and faults, and he allows us to see ourselves as we are, without the masks we normally wear. All the opinions and abuses and approvals of others melt away in the presence of God, and they cease to have their hold on us the more time we linger with him. Solitude draws us deeper into the heart of God and loosens the bonds of fear in us.

In childbirth, few women are left to true solitude. A laboring mother may be in the presence of a husband, a doula, midwives, nurses, or doctors. In labor, being alone is rarely ideal—women often want and need the comfort and help of caring companions who will allow her to focus on the hard work of labor. We can cultivate an inner sense of solitude as we practice this discipline more, setting up an "inner sanctuary in the heart," as Richard Foster calls it[21]—an ever-abiding awareness of God's presence and activity as we go through the day. Solitude creates space in our hearts and minds for meditation and prayer.

Meditation

When we think of meditation, we often imagine a Buddhist sitting in the lotus position, chanting and emptying his mind, detaching himself from the natural world. Meditation is popular among New Age practitioners, but the biblical writers were meditating long before it became the subject of expensive seminars. In biblical meditation, a person ruminates on God's nature and deeds, on Scripture, on God's creation, and on events as they relate to God, among other things. Christian meditation does not seek to empty the mind but pushes aside distractions to be filled up with God. In meditation, we seek understanding and engagement with God so that we can live more faithfully and attentively in the world. Christian meditation is based in a belief that God interacts with us as we move through life.

We tend to skim what we read, check our smartphone notifications constantly, and get our news and updates from friends in quick sound bites. Even our devotions might be one-minute thoughts with a quick prayer tacked on. We need to slow down, stop multitasking, and drink deeply of God. When we spend intentional, undistracted time with God, we are able to see him more clearly. Meditation is neither a cerebral exercise nor something to give you merely emotional warm fuzzies—it involves the whole person. You do not turn off your brain or ignore whatever is going on in your heart or disconnect yourself from your body. In meditation, our brains begin to think more deeply about God, our hearts sort through the mess of emotions and join to his heart, and our bodies calm down from the frenzy of our fast-paced lives. In this way, meditation is perfect for childbirth, since labor also engages our emotions, thoughts, and bodies in the deepest ways.

Meditation during labor can help you center your whole being on Christ, become attentive to his work in your womb, and receive the peace that comes from being in his presence. Childbirth takes an increasing amount of focus for the mother—she goes from chatting between contractions to zoning out as she works hard with her body as delivery nears. If a mother's focus is on the noise outside or the bustling of medical staff or where her pain is on a scale of 1 to 10, she may become fearful. If, however, she is meditating on God and his Word, she can be attentive to the ways he is imparting peace and working for her good. It is a good idea to practice meditation throughout your pregnancy so that you will be able to focus well during labor, where you will likely have many distractions you will need to block out.

Prayer

Prayer is so simple that it feels complicated. We have full and instant access to God through Jesus, our high priest. We don't need the right words, the right posture, the right place, or even the right motives. God knows us, and he is not fooled when we play dress up with our prayers. When we pray, we reach out for this great God to come into our lives, to show us where he already is. We interact with him and converse with him, confident that he not only exists but he also listens, cares, moves, and changes things. Even when we don't feel his presence with us, we know that he is there. During those times when he seems most absent, we have the opportunity to grow in prayer without the emotional crutches we sometimes rely on rather than God himself.

What's more, God *desires* this interaction with us. He wants us to come to him with our gratitude, doubts, fears, confessions, worship, adorations, and frustrations. These are the things relationships are made of. As we pray we are drawn into that relationship with God, and "we all, who with unveiled faces contemplate the Lord's glory, are being transformed into his image with ever-increasing glory, which comes from the Lord, who is the Spirit" (2 Cor 3:18). Praying also keeps us in tune with what is happening inside us—which we often avoid. If during an argument with my husband I pray about it, suddenly I see my anger, my pride, and my hurt. I'm forced to acknowledge what is in me. While I could complain to a friend and allow myself to remain a victim, if I pray to an all-knowing God about it, he shows me the true measure of things. Sometimes I cannot think clearly about things until I have prayed about them.

During labor, we may feel out of control, fearful, or unable to think clearly. We need the practice of submitting ourselves fully to God in prayer, because prayer reminds us that God is there to listen to us and to help us out of his great love for us. Prayer allows us to acknowledge fear and submit it to God, rather than hiding it and allowing it to remain in us.

Exercises for Solitude, Meditation, and Prayer

1. Set aside 30 minutes for meditation and prayer in solitude. If you have young children, you may have to coordinate with your spouse, a friend, or a relative to give you uninterrupted time, or do this while your children sleep. Turn off your phone and all technology and place yourself outside or in a room as free from distraction as possible. Breathe deeply with your hands on your belly, preparing your body to slow down. With your palms up, invite God to join you and sit for a few minutes in silence, listening and being attentive. Create the inner space of true solitude so that you can meditate and pray.

2. Choose a passage of Scripture to meditate on, from a Bible without study notes if you are distracted easily. Limit the passage in size, considering each word slowly and listening for what God is saying in his Word. Do not rush. The point is not to dissect the theology but to encounter God through his Word, listen, and obey. The psalms are a great starting point for meditation. Carefully read each word, allowing images and your imagination to fully engage with the passage. Read the passage several times very slowly, with a listening spirit. Ask God to teach you from his Scriptures through his Spirit. Your body is an important part of this process. If your muscles are tense or uncomfortable, you may be hindering your receptivity to God and his work in you. Relax your muscles, sit comfortably, and breathe deeply. Your posture, muscle tension, and your breathing are all important aspects to control during childbirth, too; tense muscles or holding your breath may make labor more painful and slow. If you are preparing for labor, you might choose passages of Scripture a few weeks before and write them on index cards or print them artistically to use as a focal point for labor. You could even record someone reading the chosen passages so that you can listen to them during labor (it may be easier to listen rather than read during labor).

3. Put your hands on your belly and imagine God knitting your child together in your womb. Think of all the intricacies and

the intimacy of this work. Let prayers of gratitude, worry, praise, petition, or whatever is in you flow out unhindered. Ask God to show you his glory through pregnancy and childbirth.

4. Use your imagination to create a birth scenario in which you sense God's presence and love for you as you labor and give birth, knowing that God designed and created childbirth. Pray for any concerns about childbirth and hindrances you may perceive to your birth scenario, asking God whether it is realistic and how to make it happen.

5. Remind yourself of your own story of God's work in your life. Consider writing it down in a journal. How do this pregnancy, birth, and new baby fit into that tapestry? Meditate on God's great love for you, his mercy, and milestones in your life where you saw him working—or where you still don't understand what he was doing. Pray your gratitudes, your disappointments, your sadness, and your joy to God. Maintain a listening posture, as God often gives us insight as we prayerfully reflect on our past.

6. Consider instituting a daily time-out for solitude with God. If you have young children, you may find this a challenge, but it is one worth taking on for the sake of you and your children. Even if you can only find 10 or 15 minutes when your children are distracted or asleep, use those precious minutes to settle your mind and your body into the quiet for prayer and just being with God. Leave your cell phone or other technology in another room so that you are not drawn to distractions. Breathe deeply and listen. Check in with your heart and pray for forgiveness, strength, or whatever it is that you need from him in this moment.

CHAPTER 2

Image-Bearers of the God Who Gives Birth

Nothing, however insignificant, could be credited to God's creature without also seeing it as the work of the giving God.

–Kelly M. Kapic, *God So Loved, He Gave*[1]

Birth Goddesses

As I thumbed through parenting magazines in the midwifery clinic, a small statue on the bookshelf caught my eye. It was a fat, squatting figure that looked vaguely like a woman, eyes bulging and head thrown back. I looked closer and realized her hands were spreading wide her vulva, and a baby's head was emerging. The nurse came through the door to call me back and laughed at my shocked observation of the bizarre statue. "It's an Aztec birth goddess," she explained. "Many women use the goddess as a focal point during labor to help them channel their own inner birth goddess for strength and power."

Inner birth goddess? "Oh, you mean the Aztecs used this as a focal point?"

The nurse furrowed her brow at my ignorance. "No. Women in *this clinic* use it. It's very empowering, knowing they carry the strength and wisdom of the birth goddess deep down. You're free to borrow it when your time comes!" I thanked her for her kind offer and declined, though intrigued.

Birth goddesses have been worshiped and called upon throughout history in many cultures to aid in fertility and childbirth. In many myths, the goddesses who held power over birth also controlled the interconnected life-giving powers of fertility, agricultural success, and rainfall. It was widely believed that worshiping and sacrificing to these birth goddesses granted success and safety in childbirth, as well as abundant crops and healthy livestock.[2] These deities represented life itself for struggling agrarian cultures. Baal and Asherah were two such deities of Canaan that wooed Israel into idol worship during biblical times. Canaanites believed if Baal and Asherah copulated, then fertility would be granted to livestock, crops, and women. To arouse them, worshipers often had sex in the temples and high places devoted to these gods. They presented offerings of slaughtered animals and even children to these gods and goddesses to secure their favor.

In her book *Rediscovering Birth*, anthropologist Sheila Kitzinger describes the birth practices of several cultures that set childbirth within spiritual narratives. These practices include prayer to various birth deities, meditation, sacrifices, charms and amulets for protection, and community practices that aid laboring women and place childbirth within a sacred story. She even describes Mary, Jesus' mother, as an early Christian version of the birth goddess:

> The spiritual nature of birth is central to Christianity. Mary's pregnancy is of God, not man. Like many of the goddesses before her, she is a virgin. She gives birth in a stable surrounded by animals, a scene in which there is an echo of the goddesses Cybele and Artemis. Like the birth goddesses before her, the Virgin Mary protected women in childbirth. In the 16th century, Catholic women in England wore a special sash, the Girdle of Mary, in pregnancy and birth, or a woman in labor might wear her own girdle once it had been wrapped around a sanctified bell.[3]

Of course, this depiction of Mary as a goddess is not what the biblical authors intended, but practitioners of secular traditions merged their childbirth practices with Christian beliefs. Some of these images may not have been worshiped but instead used as focal images during labor to give confidence to a mother. Midwife Ina May Gaskin describes her use of the *sheela-na-gig*, a birthing figure carved into ancient church doorways in the British Isles and as figurines found in monasteries. These figures often showed a female figure squatting, holding open wide her vagina as a baby emerged. Gaskin hypothesizes that these figurines were used "to quell the fears that young women can have when they are unable to imagine how their baby can be born. A visual image seems to help some women give birth more easily."[4] In a day where women are too often told that their babies are too big to be born naturally, it can be helpful to instill confidence that the female body was made to open wide for a baby's passage. The use of these images as a focal point rather than as objects for worship is probably more prevalent in the United States, but sometimes the line between trusting in an image and being inspired by it becomes blurred.

Fertility and birth deities are not simply relics of ages past. Modern Western culture embraces "the goddess within" narrative as a method of empowering laboring women. Many mothers rightly exchange the "damsel in distress" motif for something more courageous, and childbirth is a prominent battleground in this war. The modern medical model of birth often has the mother lying on her back, waiting for the knights in white to rescue her from her own body with an epidural and forceps. Too often, women are recipients of unforeseen and often unwanted interventions, with experts commanding obedience for the sake of the child. Many mothers are weary of this passive role in childbirth and want to take back their role as strong deliverers of life.

Unfortunately, the women who lead the conversation on strong, empowered birth also frequently teach the "mother goddess" myth. Even if they don't truly believe in birth deities, the general teaching is for a women to look within herself for power, wisdom, and strength to overcome fear and pain in labor, ultimately setting herself up as a deity to be trusted for wisdom and deliver-ance. Mothers in labor are portrayed as demigoddesses who need no one, who are sufficient in themselves, who have inner wisdom that can be tapped into and released by fervent soul-searching.

Sacredness in Childbirth

While I don't agree with practices that seek to manipulate birth deities into providing a positive birth experience or those that en-throne mere creatures as goddesses, the prevalence of these sto-ries and practices shows the common human understanding that something sacred happens at birth. While we desperately need to be reminded of the potential strength and endurance of pregnant and laboring women, this view needs to be tempered with a realis-tic picture and, for Christians, a more robust theology of woman-hood and childbirth. What we believe about God comes out in our birth practices, in our emotional state during labor and postpar-tum, and in our actions as we parent our children.

How should Christians, who reject New Age birth-goddess empowerment, approach birth as followers of Jesus? Our view of God must color and inform all of our practices, including our birth practices. But few women know how our Christian faith embeds us within a long, sacred story that gives meaning and depth to what happens at childbirth.

Christ-centered childbirth is not an alternative birth goddess story with a Christian slant; this is the ultimate story of the God of birth, and it looks radically different from the typical birth-deity narrative. As Margaret Hammer writes:

> The church offers a context, a story in which the expe-rience of childbirth can be understood and articulated: Its words of praise and lament are rooted in the mul-tifaceted drama of God's ongoing involvement in the world. Within its first few chapters, the Bible reflects on the paradoxical coinciding of suffering and joy at the birth of a child. Less familiar Bible passages, too, like those in which God is depicted as giving birth, may

lend new meaning to the human experience of birth. In addition, the church's varied efforts to comprehend the mystery and miracle of birth through the ages offer perspectives for today.[5]

During my third pregnancy, I read many "empowered birth" books that encouraged me to embrace my strength as a mother and reject the idea that pregnant women are fragile. While careful to reject the goddess narrative, I planted myself within the story of strong women who bring life. It affected the way I viewed myself. I lifted my toddlers more, I played harder, I worked harder, and as a result, I noticed that I was stronger and felt better in the last weeks of my third pregnancy than I had during my first two pregnancies. I was amazed at the abilities of my hugely pregnant body, most of all in childbirth as I brought my daughter to the world in strength and fearlessness.

However, while I was physically stronger, the mother goddess narrative also loaded guilt and shame on me when I felt the limitations of my own body. Pregnant mothers *do* have limits, and the limitations are greater than the limitations on bodies of non-pregnant women. As my belly expanded and my growing daughter filled me up and weighed me down, I found myself out of breath, out of energy, and unable to walk or sit for long periods. My back ached, though I had worked hard to strengthen my muscles throughout the pregnancy. My ankles swelled and I developed varicose veins, forcing me to wear compression pantyhose in the Texas heat to help with circulation. As I neared labor, my so-called inner goddess couldn't be paged. I was coming to terms with my own humanity. These books left me almost unable to admit my creaturely weaknesses and limitations. And I still had postpartum ahead of me! I felt as if I lived in a paradox: A pregnant woman is strong, and a pregnant woman is weak.

My pregnancies were also healthy, so the birth goddess/strong mother story seemed more possible for someone like me. But what of those who don't have healthy pregnancies and deliveries? Are they less worthy "birth goddesses" when their blood pressure spikes and they are put on mandatory bed rest? What of my otherwise perfectly healthy friend from college who inexplicably bore two micro-preemies? Did she not summon up her goddess well enough, or—to put a Christian spin on it—did she not have enough faith in God?

While we are not birth goddesses with infinite power and strength available if we just believe hard enough, we Christians worship the ultimate God of birth. Pregnancy and childbirth can bring us to worship him and even imitate him as women who bear his image—in our strength, in our weakness, in our suffering, and in our fierce mother love. And our birth practices should reflect our view of him.

God Our Mother?

Christians worship Yahweh, the creator of the heavens and the earth, the one who is life and gives breath to every creature, the sustainer and provider. In an often-ignored theme, Scripture also describes Yahweh using the image of a birthing and nursing mother. These metaphors tell us something about the heart and nature of God, and they provoke our imaginations: Our God will not be contained within our conceptions and categories.

There seems to be great fear within evangelical circles, in particular, around the concept of God as Mother. The church would do well to scrutinize these fears—especially since the Bible, which we believe is inspired by the Holy Spirit, contains passages describing God in feminine terms. We cannot ignore these passages; they tell us about the God we worship. We cannot look away from the passages that would challenge us simply because they make us uncomfortable. On the other hand, a full pendulum swing is not the answer either; some feminists so balk at the prevalence of masculine language in the Bible that they opt to call God "Mother" rather than "Father" and refer to God as "she" rather than "he." It's true—the Bible has been abused as a basis for exploitation and subordination of women at times throughout history. But conversations about God's femininity (or discussions on gender in the church at all, for that matter) can quickly dissolve into caricatures, shouting matches, sarcasm, or simple dismissal of what the other side is saying.

We are, as a culture, more comfortable with depictions of God in male terms. We may balk when some refer to God as she or Mother, deriding them as feminists (the evangelical f-word). But we need to be careful and clear in our assumptions about God, gender, and sexuality. Do we think God *is* male? Do we imagine God with male reproductive organs, a beard, and a hairy chest? Genesis 1 tells us that all humans (male and female) are made in God's image. If male and female are both created in God's image (and thus men are not created *more* in God's image than women), then we need to envision a God who somehow is *imaged* by both sexes together and yet *goes beyond* the sexes. He is "suprasexual,"[6] a term coined by Adrian Thatcher, meaning that God is beyond sexing and is imaged in both male and female sexuality. Thatcher defines it this way: "When applied to God, the term means that God is more than, not less than, sexual. God is beyond the distinction between male and female. The image of God may be found in men and women alike."[7] This frees us from the representation of God as an "old man," made in our image, and liberates us to worship a God truly beyond our comprehension and categories.

It's true that God is incarnated in the man Jesus, but he was also a poor, Jewish, Near Eastern person during the first century. We can't suppose that the circumstances he imposed upon himself in his fully human experience make up the entirety of who God is. God subjected himself to the limitations of a human body. Although all-knowing and all-powerful, he submitted himself to a human body that had to sleep, eat, grow, and learn. Humans are created as sexual beings. God, though suprasexual, submitted himself to a human body with male sexual organs. So we can assert that while Jesus is both 100 percent God and 100 percent human, and while God uses human characteristics to describe himself throughout Scripture, his humanness doesn't somehow superimpose a particular sex upon a suprasexual God.

This is important in light of our discussion of the fertility cults that have been prevalent in many cultures throughout history.

Broadly summarized, fertility cults stemmed from the belief that the sexual lives of the gods affected the natural world, causing or allowing creation to reproduce. Margaret Hammer notes, "A biblical writer who described God as a 'she' as well as a 'he' would have risked suggesting that Israel's God was not one, but a couple."[8] The sex lives of these gods were manipulated through sacrifices, chants, magic, prayers, and even temple orgies and prostitution. The God we worship, however, does not need sex and does not have sex to create, and he certainly isn't manipulated by our efforts. He creates by the spoken word. Even as he caused Mary to conceive, the Holy Spirit "overshadowed" her; he did not have sex with her.[9] God is beyond human sexuality.

It is also true that Jesus called God "Father." This isn't so much a term of sexual origin as it is a term of *relationship* between God the Father and God the Son, as well as a relationship between God and us. "Father"—a term that once meant rejection, earning love, and harshness to me—is now redefined for me in God, who loved, accepted, and adopted me. His parenthood would be well described as Mother, too. While motherly language for God is used far less frequently in Scripture than fatherly language, it still exists within biblical tradition and is valid. These parental descriptions are meant to tell us something about God, not to define all of his parameters.

This is not a claim that has arisen recently, coinciding with the rise of feminism. Christian writers and theologians throughout Christian history, especially the monastics of the Middle Ages, latched onto depictions of God that used motherly images. In the fourth century, Gregory of Nyssa wrote, "Both terms [mother and father] mean the same, because the divine is neither male nor female."[10] Bernard of Clairvaux ascribed the breast-focused imagery in the Song of Solomon to the nourishing spiritual breasts of Christ, who feeds the Church. Julian of Norwich, an English mystic, described Jesus in her *Revelations of Divine Love* (1395) as the Divine Mother. Writing on the Black Plague that devoured Europe, Julian countered popular contemporary theology that taught the horrific plague was a manifestation of God's wrath and anger. Rather, she spoke of God's mercy, compassion, and love. Anselm wrote, "O Saint Paul, where is he that was called nurse of the faithful, caressing his sons? Who is that affectionate mother who declares everywhere that she is in labor for her sons? Sweet nurse, sweet mother, who are the sons you are in labor with and nurse, but those whom by teaching the faith of Christ you bear and instruct?"[11] This language shouldn't strike us as strange if we believe that women bear the image of God along with men. Women teach us something about God (as men do), and they represent him as they labor, give birth, and mother their children.

Image-Bearers

Genesis describes this image-bearing very simply:

> So God created mankind in his own image,
>> in the image of God he created them;
>> male and female he created them (Gen 1:27).

Both the humans are made in God's *image*, one of the words later used for *idols* that Israel erected and worshiped. Notice how important the creation of humans in Yahweh's image, as his idols, was for the Israelites. Israel was often tempted to form representations of God that were nothing like God: the idols could not move, had no creative power, did not emote, and had eyes that did not see and ears that did not hear. They were nothing like Yahweh; humans are. God commanded Israel not to form images of Yahweh because *they themselves* were images of Yahweh. God blessed his images, saying, "Be fruitful and increase in number; fill the earth and subdue it. Rule over the fish in the sea and the birds in the sky and over every living creature that moves on the ground. ... I give you every seed-bearing plant on the face of the whole earth and every tree that has fruit with seed in it. They will be yours for food" (Gen 1:28–29). In multiplying, they would fill the earth with Yahweh's idols, thereby representing Yahweh to all creation and giving him glory. Sometimes ancient kings were said to have the "divine image," and they would place statues around their domain to indicate whom it belonged to. "The images communicated that this territory was under the dominion of a particular deity or king whose laws were to be respected, whose fame was to be proclaimed, and who would protect those under his or her care."[12] In Israel, not just kings but all humans were to imitate God as cocreators who fill the earth, as vice-regents who were created to rule with justice and care, as God rules over all with justice and care. Humans made in the image of God were intended to act, in limited but powerful ways, like God does.

Eve notes this remarkable ability to cocreate with God as a child bearer as she gives birth to Cain. "With the help of the LORD I have brought forth a man," she exclaims (Gen 4:1). God created Eve from her husband's rib, and Eve participated in the creation of a third human. What an incredible gift to work with God in bringing new life to the world! Women work alongside Yahweh as they yield themselves as life-giving vessels when they give birth, as they groan and suffer over their children in childbirth, as they delight over their children, and as they cocreate with God. This doesn't make mothers *birth goddesses* by any means; it makes them small and limited representations of a wondrous Creator. Willingly or not, mothers in childbirth point humanity toward God, who created this incredible biological process, who is life-giver and nurturer and parent, and who himself groans and suffers over his people.

In the previous chapter, we explored the pervasive view of childbirth as a curse and the negative implications surrounding this fearful and fatalistic attitude about childbirth. God is not perpetually angry with women and seeking their punishment through each birth. Rather, childbirth is a signpost of Jesus Christ and his gospel that reminds us not only of that first sin, when pain entered the world, but also of the hope in the birth of the Redeemer, who will crush the serpent's head (Gen 3:15). Childbirth is *not* a curse; it is a beautiful representation of a life-giving, nurturing, suffering God.

Although childbirth is not a curse, there may be pain in the process. I am not claiming that if you trust God enough, all your pain will disappear in labor and your children will be healthy. But our cultural attitudes about birth have mixed with our biblical interpretation so we come into labor with the view of an angry God who punishes through birth. So we lay passively, awaiting rescue from our infirmity, gritting our teeth as we bear our curse, and ultimately submitting to birth practices that may increase our pain and fear—which we expected in the first place. We desperately need to reframe our ideas about childbirth in biblical terms, because they affect our view of God as well as our expectations of childbirth.

By ignoring the metaphors and layers of meaning in the birth process, we also risk missing what God wants to do in us as we give birth. It is entirely possible to go through a life-altering event without allowing it to change our hearts. In childbirth, a woman transforms from woman to mother. Her schedule, work, thoughts, love, sleep habits, body, and energy levels will all change. But it's possible for her to miss God's role in her transformation. She may believe that God was angry with her through labor or even absent from the entire process. Neither is true. God is our example of strength. He is our comfort, the one who suffers with us in mercy and compassion. And he is our salvation in the midst of childbirth and mothering. We know he is able to do this because he is the God who gives birth.

The God Who Gives Birth

In Deuteronomy, Yahweh is described as the one who gave birth to Israel:

> You deserted the Rock, who *fathered* you;
> you forgot the God who *gave you birth*.
>
> The LORD saw this and rejected them
> because he was angered by his sons and daughters
> (Deut 32:18–19).

In the New Testament, James writes:

> Every good and perfect gift is from above, coming down from the *Father* of the heavenly lights, who does not change like shifting shadows. He chose to *give us birth*

through the word of truth, that we might be a kind of firstfruits of all he created (Jas 1:17–18).

In both passages, God is presented as Father and Mother, first to Israel and then to the Church. The image of God giving birth may surprise us who typically call God "Father," but he is clearly portrayed with the traits of a mother, too. In the Deuteronomy passage, Moses also says that God nursed Jacob with honey from the crag (32:13). Amid heated gender debates in the church, we can miss what these passages actually tell us about God: that he is a loving and caring parent worthy of our faithfulness, that he is jealous for our love and obedience, and that he is a giver of good gifts and has our good in mind. The biblical writers aren't trying to put boundaries around God's gender; they are describing his character and nature in ways we humans will understand.

God is described as both a furious soldier and a mother in labor in Isaiah:

The LORD will march out like a champion,
    like a *warrior* he will stir up his zeal;
with a shout he will raise the battle cry
    and will triumph over his enemies.

"For a long time I have kept silent,
    I have been quiet and held myself back.
But now, like a woman in childbirth,
    I cry out, I gasp and pant" (Isa 42:13–14).

Indeed, Isaiah is full of motherhood and birth imagery, depicting Mother Zion who births and nurses Israel with abundance, with God as the midwife, and then God himself comforting Israel in the manner of a mother:

"Can a country be born in a day
    or a nation be brought forth in a moment?
Yet no sooner is Zion in labor
    than she gives birth to her children.
Do I bring to the moment of birth
    and not give delivery?" says the LORD.

"Do I close up the womb
  when I bring to delivery?" says your God.
"Rejoice with Jerusalem and be glad for her,
  all you who love her;
rejoice greatly with her,
  all you who mourn over her.
For you will nurse and be satisfied
  at her comforting breasts;
you will drink deeply
  and delight in her overflowing abundance."

For this is what the LORD says:

"I will extend peace to her like a river,
  and the wealth of nations like a flooding stream;
you will nurse and be carried on her arm
  and dandled on her knees.
As a mother comforts her child,
  so will I comfort you;
and you will be comforted over Jerusalem" (Isa 66:8–13).

Again, Isaiah compares God's care and remembrance of his people to a breastfeeding mother's love for the baby of her womb. He also acknowledges that even though some mothers do forget their babies, Yahweh does not:

But Zion said, "The LORD has forsaken me,
  the Lord has forgotten me."

"Can a mother forget the baby at her breast
  and have no compassion on the child she has borne?
Though she may forget,
  I will not forget you!
See, I have engraved you on the palms of my hands;
  your walls are ever before me" (Isa 49:14–16).

Yahweh is elsewhere compared to a fierce, protective mother bear (Hos 13:8), and Jesus compares himself to a mother hen longing to gather her chicks to herself (Matt 23:37). God is described as a tender parent who taught his children to walk, who bent down and brought this beloved child to the cheek (Hos 11:1–4). God is even described as a midwife attending a birth, bringing the psalmist out of the womb safely into the world (Pss 22:9–10; 71:6). God describes himself as having a womb: "From whose womb comes the ice? Who gives birth to the frost from the heavens?" (Job 38:29).

These are earthy images that listeners and readers would understand. We have seen mothers round with new life. We know what a mother giving birth is like, groaning and waiting and panting, enduring pain for the love of her child. We understand the tenderness and generosity of a nursing mother offering her breast to her open-mouthed, needy baby. We have seen the firm but loving hand of a mother guiding, disciplining, and teaching her children the way they should go. We see the mother's anger and pain when that child rejects her. These images of motherhood are lifted from our mundane lives and applied to God so that we can understand an aspect of his nature. These characteristics (compassion, love, nurture) are not exclusively female characteristics. They are *godly* characteristics, and because men and women image God, they display these characteristics. But certain characteristics may shine more clearly to us in some images more than others. A mother nursing her baby shows nurture, but so does a father giving fish to his sons when they ask (Luke 11:11).

Margaret Hammer notes that the Old Testament frequently describes God's work in the womb with both culturally male and female occupations. God is described as forming humans from the womb (Isa 49:5; Jer 1:5; Job 10:8). In the culture of the time, both craftsmen were unilaterally male. But God also "poured [Job] out like milk and curdled [him] like cheese, clothed [him] with skin and flesh and knit [him] together with bones and sinews" (Job 10:10–11). You are likely familiar with the psalmist's declaration that God "knit me together in my mother's womb" (Psa 139:13–14). Cooking, curdling cheese, and knitting—in addition to midwifery—were very female occupations at the time the descriptions were written. Hammer concludes, "There is, then, something of a balance between the metaphors drawn from the work of the craftsman and those drawn from the domestic sphere of preserving food and making clothing. Far from representing a masculine god's incursion into female territory, it seems that the biblical God's involvement in procreation called forth the womanly aspects of this same, multifaceted God."[13]

These are all metaphors, just as the concepts of God as Father and warrior are metaphors. These are imperfect and limited ways that people have attempted to describe an indescribable God with human language. We scratch at it, we use parables, hyperbole, and metaphors, we attempt to verbalize and understand the incomprehensible. While we don't have the whole picture of God, we do have a considerable number of descriptions to work with. These metaphors give us language about God; they tell us about his nature and character. We need not fear language that describes God in motherly or feminine terms—as women were made in God's image, femininity is defined by God, not God by femininity.

Worshiping the God of Birth

When we discover that God is not exclusively male and is also imaged in the ways women give birth and nurture their children, does it change anything? How could this possibly shape our souls?

After researching and writing this chapter for countless hours, I went cross-eyed at the computer screen. I poured some hot tea and went to the living room window, resting my eyes by looking as far as I could. Thoughts about God and gender and image-bearing swirled through my head, and as I prayed, I realized that my mind kept going back to a conception of God as a man. I couldn't help it; when I picture God in my head, I see a man. When I pray to God, I pray to a man. It's simpler that way. I can understand God better when I visualize him like this.

So I was brought to worship and awe when I realized how small my category for God can be. How little my vision of him is! And even as I write this, I wonder, "Should I say 'him'? 'Her'? 'Thou'? What kind of language do I now use for God who is beyond gender and sex?" I cannot even conceive of such a being; he is so far beyond me. My pronouns feel too small. My pronouns cannot contain such a great God!

Any metaphor for God runs the danger of confining him in such a way that we think we understand him. Mother, Father, warrior, midwife, rock, shepherd, bread, water, light, wind—these are ways people have reached for God with human words and experiences, the ways they have compared God to things they see around them, often under the inspiration of the Holy Spirit. And it's the way God has graciously revealed himself to us, using images we can comprehend, so that we can know him in a way that portrays his nearness as well as his transcendence.

When Ezekiel found himself in the presence of God, his attempt to describe what he saw looked much the same—an inadequate grasping at imagery. "High above on the throne was a figure *like that* of a man. I saw that from what *appeared to be* his waist up he *looked like glowing metal, as if* full of fire, and that from there down he *looked like fire*; and brilliant light surrounded him. *Like the appearance* of a rainbow in the clouds on a rainy day, so was the radiance around him. This was the *appearance of the likeness* of the glory of the LORD" (Ezek 1:26–28). It's as if Ezekiel is grasping for possible descriptions to convey what he saw but knows he isn't coming close. He repeats "like" and "looked like," but he can't quite nail down in human language what he sees. "The appearance of the likeness" sounds to me like "kinda, sorta maybe looks like." John has much the same experience in the opening chapters of Revelation. God is too much to describe. We need to cast wide nets for descriptions and metaphors—none of them encompass him.

We need not fear feminine descriptions of God. God gave them to us in Scripture as another way of knowing something about him. These passages convey God's compassion, his care and loving-kindness, his fierce and protective love, and his gentleness to us—his frail and needy newborns. But ultimately, they are just a few descriptions that kinda, sorta describe God without encompassing all that he is.

So what does it matter? Primarily, this vision of God affects our worship of him. Is our view of God too small? The answer is undoubtedly "yes." But it is ever expanding when we approach him as humble learners, curious about him and what he is like. And our view of God affects how we approach him. Do we stand at a distance, bracing for his anger and wrath to fall? Do we imagine him in our particular theological campsite, shaking his head along with us at those who don't have it quite right? Or do we approach God's throne of grace expectantly, seeking a good parent eager to give grace and brimming with love and longing to lead us down the right path?

We cannot spend all our time arguing about whether to call God "he" or "she" or whether it is appropriate to call God "Mother" as well as "Father." This misses the point entirely; God is not a sexual being with penis or vagina. Why have metaphors to describe what God's character is like? The passages we've discussed describe a God who is intimately involved with his people, who cares for them tenderly, who provides for their needs, who saves them from ruin. These passages tell us of a God anguished by the sins and idolatry of his people, like a woman in childbirth. Let us not miss the beauty of this God by narrowing in on the gender language and agendas. Those who embrace God as Mother and those who reject such notions can come together and adore the God who is described in the Scriptures this way.

Birth Practices That Reflect Yahweh

When we worship Yahweh rather than birth gods and goddesses, our birth practices will be distinctively different. When we have a better understanding of God, we stop seeking to manipulate a pregnancy, a certain birth outcome, or anything out of God by incantations, wishes, and doing the right things so that he will bless us with what we want. Rather, he invites us into relationship with him as our Parent. He invites honest, persistent prayer that seeks his intervention in infertility or illness, and he conforms us into his image in the wrestling. He invites us to trust him and rest in confidence in his goodness rather than try to earn his good favor or certain blessings. He gives lavishly and sometimes chooses paths for us that we would not choose ourselves, because he is a person, not a robot requiring a certain formula to get the right result. When we choose to engage with this person instead of a magic-genie god, we find we are transformed in the process, whatever the outcome.

Reflecting Yahweh as we give birth means that it is okay to be wherever you are in labor—at the brink of despair or full of joy, on the operation table or in the birthing tub, with an epidural or counting through the rise and fall of another contraction. Your "birth goddess" status depends on none of these things, because as worshipers of the true God of birth, we have grace and love in abundance. There is no pressure to have the perfect birth experience other than for your joy and comfort, because God does not view you as a failure if things go differently. You are not loved less by God or somehow cared for less by God if there is trauma during childbirth.

Birth practices that are distinctly Christian are rooted in reality, not mythology. Women are made strong because God has created them in his image. Women have limitations because they are human and not God (or goddesses!). Once we embrace our humanity, we are free to enjoy the strength God gives us and revel in the Sabbath rest given to us by our loving creator. In pregnancy and birth, power and weakness intermingle. We can have confidence that God created our bodies to birth the babies he has grown in us, while acknowledging that sometimes even a healthy body with a healthy baby needs surgical help. Perhaps our weakness in pregnancy even prevents women from arrogance in our important job of cocreating with God.

Worshiping the true God of birth means that we can cling to this mothering God who cares for us, loves us, protects us, nurtures us, and walks with us. God labors and groans for his people as we labor and groan over our children. We can identify with this God, who has given himself over to suffering and even death, as we consider the risks that childbirth sometimes brings. If we feel isolated, uncared for, or unloved, it isn't because we *actually* are; it is because we are not seeing God as he is, as he longs for us to understand him.

Glorifying God in Labor

If we are not careful, we can set up our birth plans and philosophies as idols in our hearts. We may seek to be the poster mothers for natural birth, water birth, home birth, or a particular labor management method. We may judge others who want things a different way, thinking we have achieved superiority over their way of thinking. This is a temptation throughout parenting, actually. No matter what choice you make or what choices were made for you—breastfeeding or bottle feeding, staying home or working outside the home, attachment parenting or scheduled routines, potty training at age two or three or four—these are all areas where we may feel simultaneously superior and judged. We begin to build up our identities—in pride or in shame—around the type of births we want or had and, later, around the type of mothers we become. But this is a woman's identity formed in the image of a birth goddess! If you believe you are made in the image of a birth goddess, then your birth experience defines you. You must glorify your birth experience (or live in the trauma of it) because that is how you image the god you worship.

But we are image-bearers of Yahweh, who is living and dynamic and not limited to birth. We are now free to glorify God's beautiful work in labor as we participate in creating new life. We are free to choose pharmaceutical pain relief because we know God's pleasure in us does not depend on our birth performance. We can cling less tightly to the birth we wanted and cling to Jesus in the aftermath of the birth that happened. Because Jesus is our Lord and not these birth goddesses, we bring glory to God in whatever circumstances we find ourselves in while pregnant, laboring, postpartum, or beyond. We are not the sum of our birth experiences.

When we are able to put childbirth in its proper perspective—something that glorifies God and points to Jesus—then we can let go of our categories of "success" and "failure" in birth. A friend of mine recently attempted a vaginal birth after a cesarean (VBAC), but her uterus ruptured during labor and both she and her baby were in great danger. She described it as a "failed

VBAC." She struggled for nearly a year with feelings of failure and guilt over her epidural and cesarean. I battled my own pride when I achieved a drug-free birth. Vaginal birth doesn't equal success. Drug-free doesn't equal success. We succeed when we honor Jesus, and we glorify his strength at work in us in our weakness.

The gospel is a profound antidote to both our feelings of shame and our feelings of superiority in childbirth. Because of Jesus' death and resurrection, we have been reconciled with God. We are sealed and indwelled by his Holy Spirit, making us permanent members of his household and enabling us to operate in his power. All shame has been nailed to the cross and has died with Christ, and we are raised to new life with him. We are not condemned, and God has lavished unbelievable grace on us. All superiority should melt at the feet of Jesus, who is the giver and originator of the good gifts we have, who is our strength and power, and who has loved us in our worst moments. It should humble us to join in this miraculous work of childbirth as colaborers with God and, in a way, mirror the sacrifice of Christ in love for another.

Belonging to God means, most profoundly, that our identity is not based in our role as a mother (or not a mother), or our ability (or inability) to have children. Our identity is that we are image-bearers of Yahweh, however imperfectly we represent him, and that we are being constantly transformed into the image of his Son (2 Cor 3:18; Rom 8:29). We can trust God to use our birth stories, our motherhood, our suffering, and our joy to accomplish this ever-increasing transformation. Because women are image-bearers in childbirth, we can consider our pregnancies, labors, and deliveries as acts of worship to Yahweh as we seek to imitate him in these raw, human moments. In this way, birth becomes sacred as it acts as a sign of God's character, his person, and even as a reenactment of the birth, death, and resurrection of Christ. (Chapter 5 will discuss this further.) Childbirth, considered in this way, becomes a powerful yet common image before all of humanity that proclaims God's life-giving creation, his presence, and his loving care.

When I was in kindergarten, we recited a simple prayer before meals: "God is great; God is good; let us thank him for our food." God is great: He is beyond our understanding, he is holy, he is other, and he is high above us. But God is also good: He has birthed us and nursed us, he has come near in Jesus, and he has brought us to himself. He is both near and far.[14] In the next chapter, we will explore this transcendent, high-above-us God who is also Immanuel—God with us.

Spiritual Disciplines for Chapter 2

In chapter 2, we contrasted the ancient and modern concepts of birth deities with Yahweh, the God of birth. We cannot control or manipulate him into giving us fertility or the births we desire, nor can we assume the role of birth goddesses. As women give birth, they image God by reflecting his creative power and act as coworkers with him in bringing forth new life. We also explored the suprasexual nature of God and how imagery of God as Mother should not frighten or enrage us, but instead move us into a deeper understanding of what God is like.

The spiritual disciplines for this chapter are worship, study, and rest. As our boundaries around God and his gender and nature become expanded in our hearts and minds, we are naturally driven to worship. The discipline of study also trains our minds in focusing our intellects upon God, discovering the riches of his vastness that will forever grow our understanding. Finally, the discipline of rest allows us to acknowledge our humanity and our limitations, trust in God's infinite resources, and embrace the good, God-given rhythm of work and rest.

Pregnancy, birth, and parenting color the experiences of these disciplines. It is profoundly formative to worship the Creator as your body is swelling with proof of his active creativity. Study may become more difficult with the notorious "mom brain"—but it also becomes important as you consider teaching truths to young minds. The rhythms of work and rest help us battle against exhaustion and overworking as well as sloth and unproductiveness—all common temptations in pregnancy and in parenting.

Again, please do not feel that you need to do all the exercises. Choose what you feel will be helpful to you in this season to propel you towards the God of grace, who transforms us.

Worship

When we grasp how great and transcendent God is, it leads us to the spiritual discipline of worship. And when we slip into thinking more highly of ourselves and less highly of God than we should, the discipline of worship brings us back into right thinking about God and ourselves. While we often think of worship in terms of joy, sometimes worship is a sacrificial discipline. This lack of joy doesn't make worship any less genuine; rather, bowing down to God in all of life's circumstances can be most transformative. God is worthy of our adoration and praise at all times, and this interplay of joy and discipline is especially intense during pregnancy and childbirth—an emotional, hormonal, and physical thrill ride!

In Revelation 4, John is caught up to heaven before the throne of God, where the four living creatures and the elders worship continuously. The creatures cry out:

"Holy, holy, holy
is the Lord God Almighty,"
who was, and is, and is to come (Rev 4:8).

In response, the 24 elders fall down and worship, throwing their crowns in humility before God, exclaiming:

You are worthy, our Lord and God,
to receive glory and honor and power,
for you created all things,
and by your will they were created
and have their being (Rev 4:11).

As the creatures and elders worship God, they see what we cannot yet see. We still worship in faith without having seen God on his throne in all his glory. Our minds fill in the gaps meagerly, and often we forget the magnitude of the God we worship (or sometimes, pretend to worship). When we engage in genuine worship, we proclaim God's majesty and find humility for ourselves. What are we compared with him? All of our faults and weaknesses come to light in his presence, but we know he loves us, so we experience security and freedom in this openness before God. As we worship in preparation for and even during childbirth, we are responding to what God has done and what God will do.

Worship isn't only between you and God; in Scripture, worship most often occurs in the community of the saints. While we need to abandon our fear of what others think of us, we must not ignore our neighbors during worship. When we worship together with those who are of a different race or culture or those of varying levels of education, age, socioeconomic status, and maturity, we begin to see our neighbors as God sees them. Fuller Seminary president Mark Labberton defines worship as "the dangerous act of waking up to God and to the purposes of God in the world, and then living lives that actually show it."[15] We may learn from those we didn't expect to learn from or find ways that we fill one another's needs and lacks. Community is important in the discipline of worship. We are drawn together into the heart of God and then sent out into the world together in the power of the Holy Spirit.

Study

As God's image-bearers, we need the mind of Christ to understand God and obey him better, as our understanding of God is muddled and diminished by sin. The discipline of study engages the mind in rational, careful, concentrated thought. Bible study is perhaps one of the most familiar disciplines for Christians. We tend to consider study an exercise of the mind only, but doing so without engaging the heart and body leads to unholy, arrogant people who merely look at the Word but do not do what it says. Study is the first step—we study to interpret the Bible or other works correctly, and then we must integrate our knowledge into our lives so that we gain wisdom and obey God. Study exercises our minds to endure in concentration—a skill we may lose in our multitasking and constant distraction.

Study is sometimes seen as exclusively practiced by professional theologians; indeed, the wealth of commentaries and great tomes expounding the Scriptures in their original languages can be intimidating. While we have the Holy Spirit and he brings great understanding, we also need these great minds in order to open up the historical context, ward us away from heresy and poor interpretations, and ultimately aid us in our faithfulness to the

Scriptures. As we study, we seek knowledge of the truth so that we might become more discerning, wise, and humble as we submit to the teachings of what we are studying. We must be on guard against being puffed up by knowledge—asking God for open, teachable hearts as we study.

While the Bible is the *primary* study material for Christians, it is by no means the only subject of study. Much can be learned from studying creation—after all, "the heavens declare the glory of God" (Psa 19:1). Books by wise people, especially classic books that have stood the test of time, are also quite useful for study. Here's a mix of ancient and modern authors who have written excellent works to get you started: Augustine, Dietrich Bonheoffer, A. W. Tozer, C. S. Lewis, Thomas à Kempis, G. K. Chesterton, J. I. Packer, Henri Nouwen, and Richard Foster. Reading these books can be one avenue of walking with the wise to become wise. For childbirth, reading several books by experienced birth professionals of all types can help you better understand the physiology of birth as well as the history of midwifery and obstetric care. Expanding our knowledge about pregnancy and childbirth—even from secular sources—can enrich our appreciation for God's good creation and give us insight into the marring of creation by that first sin. Studying childbirth practices can help us reflect objectively on past birth experiences or consider better approaches for managing our own care in the future as a way to honor God's creation.

Rest

When we come to an accurate view of God and ourselves through worship and study, we will finally embrace the freedom of Sabbath rest. Sabbath is commanded for God's people right alongside prohibitions against murder and setting up false idols to worship (Exod 20:3-17), yet we feel little compulsion to obey this command. Efficiency, hard work, and productivity are highly valued in Western society. Determined to fill every hour with work, many of us lead frenzied lives with very little margin. Others might intend to rest but end up frittering away their time on restless activity—checking social media sites, watching television, or whatever else they can use to fill small voids of time. Some say that Sabbath rest simply consists of not working. These days, we have to truly consider the goal of rest; so many lethargic activities allow us to sit still and yet fail to truly refresh us.

My Spiritual Formation professor in college often told his chronically sleep-deprived students, "Sleep is spiritual. Sometimes it is the most spiritual thing you can do." While many of the students took this as license for laziness or poor time management, his statement is true. Approximately one third of our lives is spent sleeping; if we do not submit our bodies to adequate rest, it stops functioning at its best. Many people believe that if they skip out on sleep they will be more productive, but the truth is that they will likely become slower and duller in the work they do. When we are tired, we have to learn to say, "I have limits, and I need to rest. Things will have to be left unfinished and imperfect because *I am not God.*" Sleep is spiritual because it forces us to acknowledge our humility and dependence upon God, and it tempers our need to control everything around us. Sufficient sleep also infuses us with the energy and stamina we need to make good decisions, work hard, and serve others—in other words, sleep is one of the things God gives us for living a godly life. Sleep is indeed spiritual!

Humans have abused God's command to rest and made it into something it was never meant to be. Imagine God's bewilderment at Israel when they took his kind and merciful command to rest and turned it into an oppressive system of laws dictating how many steps you could take, what types of people or animals you could help, or what you could carry on the Sabbath! Jesus reprimanded the Pharisees, "The Sabbath was made for man, not man for the Sabbath" (Mark 2:27). The point of Sabbath rest is not to create slavery, but to give freedom! Rest allows us the margin to rejoice in God and perceive life as it truly is—a gift from God that comes straight from his hand.

On the other hand, a day of rest was intended to follow six days of work. You cannot have rest without work. Laziness has been a vice in all times and cultures—Proverbs speaks against laziness frequently and harshly. To adequately appreciate the benefits of deep rest, we need to engage in sustained hard work. Paul tells the Colossians, "Whatever you do, work at it with all your heart, as working for the Lord, not for human masters, since you know that you will receive an inheritance from the Lord as a reward. It is the Lord Christ you are serving" (Col 3:23-24). Working for the Lord also means that our identity is not wrapped up in our work. As those who image God, our identity is in Christ.

In childbirth, the rhythms of rest and work are built into the natural progression of labor. Labor is not often like labor shown in the movies, with constant screaming and agony. God has built rest into the hard work of labor. Contractions last from about 30 seconds in early labor to about 90 seconds in duration near the end. Between these contractions, the mother is given a reprieve of anywhere from 20 minutes in very early labor, 3-7 minutes in active labor, and perhaps a minute or so between pushes at the end. The mothers who have the most satisfying labors intentionally take this time to rest their bodies and minds. During these breaks, they close their eyes, breathe deeply, and relax every muscle. It is in these periods of rest that the mother can gain strength and renewed vision for the hard work ahead.

In pregnancy, we can let our limits and weaknesses drive us to rest in God's strength and mercy. We can take time throughout each day to rest, acknowledging our weakness in order to grow in humility, and recommit ourselves to God's strength. We can rest with holy intention and rejoice in our gracious God who knows our weaknesses and is not a taskmaster with whip in hand. Our weakness can lead us to worship.

Exercises for Worship, Study, and Rest

1. Cultivate an attitude of praise and thanksgiving to God. Do this inwardly throughout the day—in your heart or in a journal. Speak your praise and thanksgiving to God in front of others as well. Marvel at God's work in your womb, through healthy checkups, over kicks and tumbles. Allow spontaneous praise to punctuate even your labor as you celebrate the passing of each contraction, the nurse attending you, the creation of epidurals,

or the ability to labor naturally. You are not a victim—you are wholly loved and cared for by God, in large and small ways.

2. Before each church service, take time to prepare yourself for corporate worship. If you had a hard night of practice contractions, cramped legs, or a cranky newborn, submit the hardship of this season to God and commit to worship him wholeheartedly through it. Come to worship expecting God's movement. Worship with your hands on your pregnant belly or around your sweet baby, recognizing that the sight of you worshiping the Creator will be one that your child will grow up learning from. Others might experience God's creative power and be drawn deeper into worship as they watch your belly grow each week.

3. Choose a book of the Bible to study deeply and slowly. Borrow or buy a commentary or two to aid your study. Make notes on what you are learning, and make a commitment to obey the Scriptures. Two great resources for learning how to study the Bible well are *How to Read the Bible for All Its Worth* by Gordon D. Fee and Douglas Stuart and *Grasping God's Word* by J. Scott Duvall and J. Daniel Hays.

4. Take time to rest each day—if you have a baby or older children, you have to be more creative about it or may need someone's help, but it is possible. Make a cup of tea or coffee, turn off the TV and set aside your phone, and leave the work/laundry/dishes unfinished. Sit quietly and enjoy the flavor of your drink. Do something that is genuinely restful—for different personalities, this will mean different things. Some ideas:

- Read a chapter of good fiction
- Sit and reflect with a journal or just your thoughts
- Have a good conversation with a close friend
- Play outside
- Create some art
- Simply sit and enjoy the quiet
- Take a nap

Resist the urge to complete a task, and celebrate the gift of rest from God.

5. Some women experience strong Braxton-Hicks contractions in the later months of pregnancy. If this is true for you, use these times to practice resting between contractions—your eyes closed, muscles relaxed, and breathing deep. It can be hard work to not focus on other things or get something done while you feel fine! This can be an opportunity to practice your resting skills for labor.

6. As you progress in your pregnancy, note the things that you cannot do comfortably any longer. Enlist the help of others. This can be difficult—it's hard to admit we need other people! People usually want to bless you but don't know how and don't want to insult you by implying you couldn't do something for yourself. Have a friend organize a meal train for postpartum, or enlist help in doing the housework. Ask God to grow humility in you as you learn to depend on others in your weakness.

7. Set aside one day a week for rest and refreshment. Use paper plates, take a nap, play with the kids, read an interesting book, take time to linger in God's Word. Resist checking email, making one more call, finishing that last bit of paperwork. Acknowledge that you have limits and that you are not God.

CHAPTER 3

The Glory and the Gory in the Incarnation

See the eternal Son of God
A mortal Son of Man,
Dwelling in an earthly clod
Whom Heaven cannot contain!
Stand amazed, ye heavens, look at this!
See the Lord of the earth and skies
Low humbled to the dust he is,
And in a manger lies!

—Charles Wesley, "Glory Be to God on High"[1]

O Holy Night

When my sister-in-law asked for a nativity scene last Christmas, I spent hours shopping online to find the perfect one. I'd like to claim selflessness fueled the search, but frankly, she would likely display this nativity scene in a prominent place in her home during the Christmas season, and I would invariably be connected to the one I chose. "You like it? Thanks, my sister-in-law picked it out!" Or conversely: "Yeah, it's pretty ugly, huh? My sister-in-law got it for me and I feel bad not putting it out." My reputation was on the line.

As I stared at the Holy Family in manger scene after manger scene, I reflected on the appearance of Mary and Jesus in particular (admittedly, with a large degree of sarcasm). I'd given birth three times. Where was *my* halo? Whereas my face was devoid of all color from blood loss and exertion after birth, Mary serenely gazed on the sweet baby Jesus (no crying he makes), with rosy cheeks and a knowing smile. I winced with the thought of kneeling next to the feeding trough with a postpartum perineum and then laughed at the thought of Mary in one of those super-sized ice-pack sanitary diapers supplied by many hospitals. I remembered all of the blood on my hospital sheets and my gown as I looked at the pristine straw in the Christmas stable.

I suddenly felt guilty for having these sacrilegious thoughts about the Christmas scene. Yet, these would have been realities for Mary. The mess of the birth, the exhaustion and work, the fear and joy mingled together as she brought from her body the Messiah, the hope of the world. And isn't all of that mess the point? That God came into the world as a true human, *the* true human? Christmas nativities, with their sanitized and glowing aura of holy birth, separate us from the messiness of real birth—of *Jesus'* actual birth.

Religious art is especially apt to wipe clean the scene of Jesus' birth. Byzantine frescoes and mosaics typically depict the Christ Child and Virgin with glowing halos, sometimes with the infant Christ giving a blessing with his hand to onlookers. Although art styles have changed through the centuries, major themes in these representations of the manger scene are holiness, adoration, light, and radiance. These themes draw attention to the uniqueness and wonder of God coming down as a human. Artists are right to convey Jesus' divinity. But there are few, if any, depictions of what the physical reality of Jesus' birth was probably like. Such depictions might connect us with his *humanity*, the most scandalous and inconceivable thing about Jesus' birth—and the point of the entire thing. The Christmas story is not primarily about God's holiness and otherness and divinity. It is profound precisely because of the humanity of it all. It is earthshaking because the high-above-us

God clothed himself in human flesh and bones, subjecting himself to the weaknesses and frailties of limited creatures, and became all at once fully God and fully man. God came near to us. And he did it through childbirth.

God set the normal process of conception and childbearing into motion in the beginning chapters of Genesis. And in the Gospels of Matthew and Luke we see God himself entering into that process as the baby. While our nativities and art may separate us from the raw humanity of the incarnation, God does not distance himself from the messiness and reality of birth.

The Word Made Flesh

There are three main players in any given pregnancy: mother, father, and baby. Within Mary's womb, God bypassed normal human conception for a supernatural one—a Trinitarian one. He foretold the birth through prophets and angels, impregnated Mary through the Holy Spirit rather than through sexual means, and was born Jesus of Nazareth, the incarnate Word of God.

The Gospel of John opens, "In the beginning was the Word, and the Word was with God, and the Word was God. He was with God in the beginning. Through him all things were made; without him nothing was made that has been made. In him was life, and that life was the light of all mankind. The light shines in the darkness, and the darkness has not overcome it" (John 1:1–5). These are lofty descriptions of our God. He is creator, he is the Word, he is eternally existent, and he is beyond all comprehension. He is the source of all life and light.

And then John makes a truly radical statement: "The Word became flesh and made his dwelling among us. We have seen his glory, the glory of the one and only Son, who came from the Father, full of grace and truth" (John 1:14). The word for "made his dwelling" in this verse literally means God pitched his tent, or "tabernacled," perhaps stirring up in the minds of the first listeners an ancestral memory of wilderness wanderings for Israel.

Closely associated with the tabernacle of the wilderness is the idea of God's glory, which he shielded from Israel and even

Moses; the full view of God's glory would have obliterated them. Leon Morris argues that John saw Jesus as the "new and greater Moses."[2] In the Exodus account, Moses begs God, "Show me your glory" (Exod 33:18). God agreed, though he had to hide Moses in the cleft of a rock and cover him with his hand as his glory passed by (33:19–23), while declaring his character: "The LORD, the LORD, the compassionate and gracious God, slow to anger, abounding in steadfast love and faithfulness, maintaining love to thousands, and forgiving wickedness, rebellion and sin. Yet he does not leave the guilty unpunished; he punishes the children and their children for the sin of the parents, to the third and fourth generation" (Exod 34:6–7). Moses was hidden from God's full glory and saw only his back and heard his voice.

But in Jesus, John says we have seen "the glory of the one and only Son, who came from the Father" (John 1:14). His tent is here. Among us—the unclean, the unholy, the unrighteous. We are unworthy of beholding God's glory and are unable to do so and live, yet we do in Jesus, "the image of the invisible God," in whom all the fullness of God dwells (Col 1:15, 19). The Word became flesh. John remarks, "No one has ever seen God, but the one and only Son, who is himself God and is in closest relationship with the Father, has made him known" (John 1:18). In Jesus, we behold the fullness and glory of God that was once hidden from us.

In addition to showing us God's glory, Jesus is the presence of God among humanity. The tabernacle was the temporary dwelling of God's presence with Israel in the wilderness. As discussed in chapter 1, the presence of God was of primary concern for Israel. For this first-century audience, God's presence was still a concern. Solomon's temple in Jerusalem, where God had dwelled in the holy of holies, had been destroyed by the Babylonians in 586 BC. The Persians had allowed the Israelites to rebuild the temple, but God's glory never filled it as with the first temple. Many wept at the opening of the new temple as they remembered the majesty of Solomon's temple. Four hundred years of virtual silence lay between the close of the Old Testament and the opening of the

New Testament. Suddenly God had restored his presence among his people—as a baby.

The Normal and the Extraordinary

The story of the incarnation is a bizarre mingling of the utterly normal and the unbelievably extraordinary. An angel visits a common peasant girl from nowhere important.[3] A virginal conception by the overshadowing of the Holy Spirit is followed by a normal pregnancy with stretch marks, kicks, and fetal hiccups. Humble hospitality is offered in a family's manger, while an unusual star marks the place. The King and Savior of mankind is born, wrapped in a simple swaddle and lying in a makeshift bed, as any other Middle Eastern baby might have been that night. Unclean, poor local shepherds and foreign, prestigious magi bearing regal gifts all come to honor the little King.

But the incarnation itself is the most unbelievable mixture of normal and extraordinary: The Creator of all took on the form of a baby and entered the womb of a young woman and was nourished by her body. God himself was squeezed by contractions in the uterus and pushed through a vagina, his head molded and misshapen by the stress of birth. He was connected to a placenta, covered in blood, and struggled for that first breath—though he himself gives the breath of life. He rooted for Mary's breast, receiving nourishment from his mother's milk though he sustains all life in the universe. The incarnation seems too normal for God, too undignified and unholy and unsanitary.

Are you cringing? The Western obsession with order and cleanliness (it's next to godliness, you know) is offended by this story. God should not be treated this way. He is too high above us, too holy, too divine! That's true—but if Jesus was a *real* human, then he subjected himself to real birth, with all its messiness and blood and trauma. God did not avoid the birth canal, the infantile dependence, and the utter humility of this part of the human life. He entered right in. His participation in the reality of birth and infancy makes the incarnation that much more incredible.

Picturing the nativity in the context of a normal human birth is startling to me. This is what birth looked like for me as I came through my own mother's body and entered the world. It's the experience I watched my own children have, with their cone heads and blood and amniotic fluid everywhere. Just as my babies did, Jesus took comfort in his mother's breast, warmth, and voice after his harsh entrance into the world. This is real birth: mess, chaos, love, pain, noise, fear, and joy. And our God entered into it purely out of love. He is Immanuel—*God with us*. And in doing so, Jesus made childbirth a hallowed time where we meet God. There is no division between sacred and secular—God has entered into every part of life.

Jesus entering so fully into humanity is part of our salvation. While modern evangelicals tend to relegate salvation only to Jesus' work on the cross, Scripture and early theologians considered Jesus' entire life to be redemptive and atoning for humanity.[4] At conception within Mary's womb, Jesus joined into the lineage of sinners— murderers, traitors, incestuous rapists—and he took on the sinful flesh of humanity without himself sinning (2 Cor 5:21) so that he could redeem it.[5] Theologians John C. Clark and Marcus Peter Johnson write, "Just as surely as Christ is our incarnate Savior and the one Mediator between God and men, he lives and acts in our place and on our behalf in all things; his birth is no exception to this rule, but the very basis and condition for it."[6] In other words, Jesus could only be a true mediator between God and humanity if his birth was a true, human birth with a true, human body. Further, the authors argue that Jesus' conception by the Holy Spirit acts as a prerequisite of sorts for our own rebirth by the power of the Holy Spirit. Jesus, through his conception and birth, fully united himself with us to heal us from the innermost parts, that we might be joined with him and find life in God.

That God has shared in all of our experiences—albeit sinlessly— through Jesus should give us great hope and confidence as we come before God. The author of Hebrews writes, "Since we have a great high priest who has ascended into heaven, Jesus the Son of God, let us hold firmly to the faith we profess. For we do not have a high priest who is unable to empathize with our weakness-es, but we have one who has been tempted in every way, just as we are—yet he did not sin. Let us then approach God's throne of grace with confidence, so that we may receive mercy and find grace to help us in our time of need" (Heb 4:14–16). God's participation in childbirth means that he is aware of our weakness as we labor. He is aware of the distress of our babies and the harsh entry into the world from the womb. He knows the danger and the fear and the exhilaration—not as an outsider who watches and takes notes on the experience, but as one who has been born as we all have. He entered in out of his great love.

Oh, that we would understand Jesus' heart for mothers and their babies as they grunt and wail and push! Jesus is one of us. He is our mediator who has fully united with us. As a mother, the incarnation is made all the more profound to me when I consider God not only authored the process of childbirth but also entered into it. That God himself participated in this work rips it from the realm of the filthy and the cursed and elevates it to the sacred.

Mary's Experience of Childbirth

We tend to relegate Mary to the background during the birth of Christ. Although it's true that she isn't the primary point of the story, she is a prominent participant in it! As a Christian who went through childbirth three times, it never occurred to me to think of Mary as an example. Perhaps if my babies had been due around Christmas, the connection might have crossed my mind. But Mary's experience of pregnancy and labor—especially her body's role in the incarnation—was the subject of many early theo-logians' wonderings.

Jennifer Glancy outlines these theological musings concern-ing Mary's laboring and postpartum body. Most early scholars derided the birthing process as "the curse of Eve" and denigrated the female body and its natural processes. Even breast milk was considered shameful, on par with excrement. Marcion, an early theologian generally regarded as a heretic for his views on the hu-manity of Christ, likened the womb to a sewer![7] For the most part, theologians seemed concerned with whether Mary maintained her virginity through the birth of Jesus (i.e., did her hymen tear during childbirth?).[8]

Some theologians posited the idea of the Immaculate Conception—later accepted as doctrine by the Catholic Church—to protect Jesus' divinity and sinlessness. This teaching holds that Mary was born without sin, so that when she carried Christ, he would not be tainted by her sin nature. Many held to the perpetual virginity as well as the sinlessness of Mary as God's vessel, and convoluted theologies with thin biblical arguments formed about the birth of Jesus. Some postulated that Mary experienced no pain in birth, since she was sinless and therefore did not receive the so-called curse of Eve and the wrath of God's anger against sin in her body.[9] According to the *Protevangelium of James*, a noncanonical book falsely attributed to James the brother of Jesus and written around AD 200, the midwife who delivered Jesus left the manger scene in disbelief at Mary's complete lack of pain and at her intact hymen after the birth. She told a passerby, Salome, who did not believe her and went to Mary to see for herself. As she put her finger into Mary's postpartum vagina, her finger burned and became leprous. Then she touched the baby Jesus and was healed of her disease. How's that for a birth story?

While these stories and theologies seek to protect Jesus' divinity from taking on human defilement within Mary's womb, they miss the point. The incarnation was the moment that Jesus fully entered into the human reality—he did not shun it or protect himself from it. We know nothing of Mary's labor and birth pains, the story from her perspective, or how her postpartum experience was. After she brings forth the Messiah, she sinks humbly into the story's background; this is *his* story after all. But Mary is a significant part of it, and God has given her honor in the role she plays in bringing the Messiah to the world. We turn now to what Scripture says about the mother of Jesus:

> In the sixth month of Elizabeth's pregnancy, God sent the angel Gabriel to Nazareth, a town in Galilee, to a virgin pledged to be married to a man named Joseph,

a descendant of David. The virgin's name was Mary. The angel went to her and said, "Greetings, you who are highly favored! The Lord is with you."

Mary was greatly troubled at his words and wondered what kind of greeting this might be. But the angel said to her, "Do not be afraid, Mary; you have found favor with God. You will conceive and give birth to a son, and you are to call him Jesus. He will be great and will be called the Son of the Most High. The Lord God will give him the throne of his father David, and he will reign over Jacob's descendants forever; his kingdom will never end."

"How will this be," Mary asked the angel, "since I am a virgin?"

The angel answered, "The Holy Spirit will come on you, and the power of the Most High will overshadow you. So the holy one to be born will be called the Son of God. Even Elizabeth your relative is going to have a child in her old age, and she who was said to be unable to conceive is in her sixth month. For no word from God will ever fail."

"I am the Lord's servant," Mary answered. "May your word to me be fulfilled." Then the angel left her (Luke 1:26–38).

My paternal grandmother is Catholic. She would play recordings of the Rosary prayers in the car, clutching her prayer beads with a free hand and reciting, "Hail Mary, full of grace, the Lord is with thee. Blessed art thou among women and blessed is the fruit of thy womb, Jesus. Holy Mary, mother of God, pray for us sinners, now and at the hour of our death, amen." She also had several Catholic cartoon videos we would watch on visits to her house, depicting famed sightings of Mary in places such as Lourdes and Fatima.

When I came into my faith as a teenager, I attended the small, conservative Southern Baptist church that my friends attended. Their view of Mary was quite the opposite from my grandmother— Mary was just a normal woman whom God happened to use, and *that's all we really need to even say about her lest we fall into worshiping her as the Catholics apparently do.* With such polarized views of Mary among the people in my life—fearing her on one side and praying to her on the other—I came to avoid her altogether. Mary was confusing for me.

And then I became a mother. I can't help but stop and wonder at Mary as I read the Gospel of Luke.

Mary: Discipleship in Motherhood

Last year, my family and I moved to a small town in the Middle East, where we are studying the language and culture and working to start a business. Living in the Arab world has given me a fresh appreciation for Mary, whose culture would have been much closer to this one than my own American culture. Here, honor and shame determine everything. I do not talk to men in public, even good friends, because it might appear too friendly to others, and appearance is everything. Here, family history and heritage are a person's identity rather than their vocation as a single individual. In the United States, I would introduce myself as Aubry Smith—a writer, childbirth educator, and doula. To my Arab friends, I am not Aubry Smith; I am Umm-Breckon, the mother of Breckon (my oldest son), wife of Brady. We see this kind of emphasis on family line in the culture of biblical characters as well—it's as if they couldn't make sense of an individual apart from their family heritage.

An honorable reputation is everything in the Middle East, especially since a person's identity is bound up with their family and community, and community shame is the end of a person, especially for a woman. If you are shamed no one will marry you and tie their name to yours, no one will come to your house or invite you into theirs, and no one will fix your car or provide favors for you because everything is relational. Nothing is "just business." You are not first and foremost an individual; you are a member of the community first, and you must bring honor and not shame to the community. And in some cases, killing the source of shame restores honor to the community.

Here is Mary, a young girl who is told by an angel that she will become pregnant by the Holy Spirit. It is almost certain no one will believe her. According to understandings of the Jewish law at that time, she might have been stoned to death for adultery because of her threat to the community (John 8:2–11). Joseph would most certainly expose her and divorce her, shaming her in the community and condemning her to a life of singleness and, therefore, poverty.[10]

What does Mary say to the angel as she faces this future of shame and possible death by bearing the Son of the Most High to the world? "I am the Lord's servant. ... May your word to me be fulfilled" (Luke 1:38). Mary's humility before the Lord, her submission to his plans for her, and her trust in God are incredible. Her Magnificat, exalting God for his mercy, is one of my favorite passages of Scripture:

> My soul glorifies the Lord
>   and my spirit rejoices in God my Savior,
> for he has been mindful
>   of the humble state of his servant.
> From now on all generations will call me blessed,
>   for the Mighty One has done great things for me—
>   holy is his name.
> His mercy extends to those who fear him,
>   from generation to generation.
> He has performed mighty deeds with his arm;
>   he has scattered those who are proud in their inmost
>   thoughts.
> He has brought down rulers from their thrones
>   but has lifted up the humble.
> He has filled the hungry with good things
>   but has sent the rich away empty.
> He has helped his servant Israel,
>   remembering to be merciful
> to Abraham and his descendants forever,
>   just as he promised our ancestors (Luke 1:46–55).

Mary is a model for us of sacrificially surrendering our bodies to God in trust and submission as we bring new life into the world. She accepts God's plan for her, though it potentially would be very risky, to bear the Messiah. Mary worships God for his goodness and his blessing to her and for his faithfulness in his promises, even if it costs her everything. She accepts the honor that God has given her, rather than the shame that will likely come from her people. Perhaps the root of Mary's humility and willingness is her grasp of the ancient hope presented here by the angel. Gabriel tells her that her son will be the long-awaited descendant of David, and in her worship, she praises God's faithfulness to his promise to Abraham and his descendants, not just to David. Mary is recognizing the fulfillment of God's long promise to Abraham:

> I will make you into a great nation,
>   and I will bless you;
> I will make your name great,
>   and you will be a blessing.
> I will bless those who bless you,
>   and whoever curses you I will curse;
> and all peoples on earth
>   will be blessed through you (Gen 12:2–3).

Thousands of years after the promise was made, here at last is the One through whom all the world will receive blessing. Here is the One who will make a great nation out of little, oppressed Israel, though not in the expected way. Here, at last, is the culmination of all of Israel's history and longing and hope: the Savior. When we, like Mary, are able to see God's long story from Eden to glory, we finally see our own place in it and begin to rightly see ourselves— and the risks God may ask us to take. Our own plans for our small lives are put into perspective. Submission to God's purposes becomes a joy and an honor, because we are flabbergasted that we have any part in them at all. Mary likely considered all that she was being asked to give up in this moment. Her willingness to say yes to God and his unfolding plan shows that she had God's long-range redemptive purposes in view.

Luke later tells us a bit more about Mary's future experience as the mother of the Son of God and the great cost she will bear. The prophet Simeon cryptically tells Mary as she presents Jesus in the temple, "This child is destined to cause the falling and rising of many in Israel, and to be a sign that will be spoken against, so that the thoughts of many hearts will be revealed. *And a sword will pierce your own soul too*" (Luke 2:34–35). Simeon foreshadows the piercing of Jesus' side on the cross, ultimately confirming his death. Mary would be there at the cross, perhaps having known all along that this might happen. But she was still a mother, and Jesus was still her son. Could anything pierce a mother's soul like the horror of watching her child tortured and killed? Kenneth Bailey writes:

> On Golgotha, Mary chose to remain to the end and witness the suffering of her son until his death. She was not under arrest and could have walked away. She knew she could not change what was happening before her by arguing with the soldiers or pleading with the high priests. The only decision she was free to make was to choose to remain and enter into Jesus' suffering. Indeed, a sword passed through her heart, and in the process, once again, she became a model for Christian discipleship.[11]

Mary's willing and even joyful submission to God's calling in childbirth and mothering are a model for us both in labor and in life. I want to follow Mary in sacrificially loving others— my children, my husband, my neighbors, and my enemies—even if a sword pierces my soul, too. If all I do is stay at the foot of someone's cross when everyone else leaves, and enter into the suffering of those in pain, let that be my lot.

Submission and Release in Childbirth

In childbirth, we have a visceral metaphor for releasing ourselves to God for his use and our good. As each contraction rises, a mother has two options. She can grit her teeth and fight it, holding her breath and digging in her heels to push with everything she has against the pain, with the mind-set that pain is bad, pain should be avoided, and pain is the enemy. When she finds she cannot make the pain go away—and worse, it keeps coming harder and faster—she may be overcome by fear. This creates a biological reality: an adrenaline response. Stress, pain, and fear can ramp up the fight-or-flight hormone response that is designed to help us manage dangerous situations. Our muscles tighten, our hearts race, and our bodies prepare for danger. A body in labor protects the mother in the face of perceived danger by prolonging labor so she can get to safety. The cervix may slow its opening or even close tighter, making labor stop or last longer. Further, tight muscles lead to more pain, creating more fear, and—you guessed it—more adrenaline. It's a vicious cycle.[12]

The other option a mother has seems much scarier at first: releasing herself to the process of contractions and managing her fear response. Rather than fighting each contraction as it comes, the mother focuses on relaxing every muscle in her body, from forehead to pelvic floor to toes. She submits herself to the process of birth, trusting that even though there is pain, it is there for a purpose and it will not overcome her. For the Christian, this trust and submission is not placed in the body, which may or may not work correctly; they are placed in God, who cares for and loves the mother. As each contraction is managed with a sense of release and love instead of fight or flight, the opposite of the adrenaline reaction occurs: More oxytocin is released by the body, creating a sense of safety, love, and best of all—a speedier birth.

Pregnancy involves releasing control and careful plans over to God's divine providence. Each month, a woman's menstrual cycle presents her with two possibilities: more of the same if her egg is not fertilized, or an entirely new life. For many couples, conception comes as a surprise, especially if they used birth control methods. The truth is, no method except full abstinence gives a couple full control over conception. Other couples feel their lack of control when they cannot get pregnant, no matter how hard they try. There is submission as women yield their bodies to pregnancy and its extraordinary physical and emotional changes. In pregnancy, parents submit themselves to the risk of miscarriage or disability; we cannot keep babies in the womb or help them develop by sheer will. Then we birth a new creature, who will be not entirely under our control (which will become more apparent in the toddler years and teen years!). We can desire them to do good and do what we want, but in the end, we cannot control them or their personalities. We give birth at great risk for our carefully planned courses of life!

Mary's response to God in the face of an uncontrollable future is consistently one of humility and submission, at great personal cost and great blessing. We join her story as we travail in hope and in our growing trust of God's goodness. Mary can rejoice as she does because she understands the character of the God who places a baby in her womb and who walks alongside her as she delivers and mothers the Son of God.

Humility and Submission in the Incarnation

The gospel is beautiful because of the God at the center of the story. Humanity turned from God, and even God's chosen Israelites repeatedly turned their trust and hearts to idols. At the close of the Old Testament, Israel split into two warring factions, and God used sinful empires like the Assyrians and Babylonians as judgment on Israel's wickedness. Then there were 400 years of God's silence and enemy occupation—centuries of whispered hopes and remembered prophecies of a coming King who would overthrow the rulers.

And then *God himself* came. Unexpectedly, God entered the womb of a peasant woman, subjected himself to normal birth, and was nursed at his mother's breast. God-in-flesh toddled around on unsteady legs and bruised his knees. The Creator and Sustainer of all living felt extreme hunger and maddening thirst that many of us reading this book won't have experienced outside of a voluntary fast. He felt the sting of rejection and the loneliness we all feel deeply at times. He entered into our mess, our filth, our pain, our indignity, and our limits. He subjected himself to it for his love of us. God's nearness to us as Immanuel—God with us—is the most incredible thing that ever happened.

The apostle Paul urged the Philippians to love in humility as an imitation of the incarnate Christ:

> In your relationships with one another, have the same
> mindset as Christ Jesus:
> Who, being in very nature God,
>   did not consider equality with God something to be used
>   to his own advantage;
> rather, he made himself nothing
>   by taking the very nature of a servant,
>   being made in human likeness.
> And being found in appearance as a man,
>   he humbled himself
>   by becoming obedient to death—
>   even death on a cross! (Phil 2:5–8).

The incarnation is God coming down into what is utterly human. The incarnation is a reminder that God does not only wait for us in marble temples or buttressed cathedrals; rather, he is present with us in the ordinary, the gross, and the everyday mess and beauty we wallow in. He has come near in the most incredible way to bring new birth. How can we imagine the love of a God who would not only give himself over to a cross but also to a woman's womb and birth canal?

The incarnation is God with us. Is there any part of our lives God does not enter, that he will not meet us in? I find it all so beautiful that I want to follow Jesus right into his incarnational life. I want the courage to step out of my comfort and safety and enter into the sufferings and hardships of others. I want to take on his humility, love others with the energy and care that I love myself with, and begin to think about myself less than I do. And it is entirely appropriate that I should do these things, because believers are not just following Jesus as an example but are *joined with Christ*. When we confess faith in Jesus, we are melded into a union with him as we take on his life.

Though I don't carry the Son of God in my womb, I want to follow Mary in submitting myself to him—whether in pregnancy or at work or in mothering or whatever I do—with the joyful attitude that says, "I am the Lord's servant." Mary gave up her desire to have her own way and chose God's way at great cost. I am struck by her trust in God's care for her in the face of dishonor and scandal; the anxiety of pregnant women is high enough without having the awkward "I promise I'm still a virgin—this is actually God's baby" talk with your neighbors. When one of Jesus' female followers cried out, "Blessed is the mother who gave you birth and nursed you," Jesus responded to her, "Blessed rather are those who hear the word of God and obey it" (Luke 11:27–28). Mary truly was blessed among women for her role as the mother of Jesus; her son is not slighting her here. But the even greater blessing comes from listening to him and following him.

Specifically in the context of pregnancy and childbirth, we have the opportunity to submit to God's loving care for us many times over. We can lean into his compassion during contractions. We can retrain our minds against the lie that he is angry with us and has cursed us, and receive his love and redemption. We can surrender our bodies to possible pain and suffering, rather than fighting our way through, trying to somehow avoid pain (and unintentionally making things worse).

Submission can be a harder task for some of us than others. We submit our anger with God to him when the pregnancy test is negative again and again, reminding ourselves that he does hear our prayers and that he is near. We submit our hopes and plans for the future to the Lord when those hopes are changed or perhaps dashed by unexpected pregnancy, miscarriage, stillbirth, or disability. We can submit ourselves to the Lord for healing rather than hanging on to wounds and bitterness if our births go the way we didn't want. God's will involves wholeness for mothers and babies—mind, body, and soul. These sufferings listed above are distortions of God's good creation, warped and muddled by sin. We can accept that suffering is now integrated into our lives and submit ourselves to him in hardship to transform us by his grace.

We can cling to our great high priest, who knows the heavy weight of suffering as we do, because he came down to us and experienced it too. We can also choose to resist his work in us as we suffer, and we must be aware of the danger in submitting ourselves to anger rather than to a loving God.

Bodies and Celebration

When I consider God's careful attention over childbearing—over the way he formed me in my mother's womb and the way he put my children together in mine—I want to honor his creative power in all of it. But I look down at the lower-belly sag that crunches and cardio can't seem to get rid of. I touch the stretch marks that my firstborn gave me in abundance. My breasts have changed with the filling and emptying of milk, and they are now losing a battle with gravity. My hips are forever widened by the bodies that passed through them. There are soft, mushy parts of me that seem to hang on to hope that I will need the fat to sustain more lives *in utero*. It's easy to give into self-destructive talk about my postnatal body. It's easy to shame the unsightly parts and grimace at the mirror on my way to the shower. If I am honest, I'm far too prone to thinking about what childbirth has done to my body and worrying about how—short of a time machine—to get my prebaby body back.

I want to hold in honor this changed-by-childbearing body that God has created, that God allowed to be fertile, that God used to create and nurture and sustain three little lives. I want to cherish this body that in some mysterious way has imaged the God who created it in the bringing of new life. Our prudishness often prevents us from deeply considering God's creative power in the female reproductive system. God made vaginas, and he did a great job on them! Episiotomies—surgical cuts made in the vagina toward the anus to make more room for an emerging baby—came into fashion in the last century as a way of mending what was "broken." Studies have shown that routine episiotomies are not only unnecessary but can cause more harm than natural perineal tears that happen in birth. God made vaginas to stretch to incredible proportions and then to return to a normal state that can hold something as small as a tampon! If you have never seen a vaginal birth, you really should find a birth video and marvel at God's genius creation. Vaginas are incredible.

The uterus is another marvelous creation by God. It is a tiny organ that balloons out to the size of a watermelon—bigger, in cases of multiple babies. The uterus is a muscle, and with powerful contractions, it is able to gently yet powerfully push a baby down into the birth canal. These contractions are actually good for the baby—besides bringing the baby into the world, they help squeeze the fluid out of his lungs, enabling that his first breath after birth. Within the uterus, a baby is nourished by an organ called the placenta, which looks like a little tree of life. This placenta will be the baby's companion, allowing her to receive nourishment from her mother as she grows and develops. The cervix is a strong combination of muscle and tissue at the mouth of the uterus that keeps the baby safely in the womb until the birthday draws near. As the baby grows closer to birth, the cervix begins to soften and open wide enough for the widest part of the baby to pass through. Thank God for the cervix!

Even our menstrual cycles are part of God's good creation, and we should thank God for them (seriously!). We are used to fighting against our menstrual cycles—we medicate them to make them more regular, less painful, or to go away entirely. If we don't want babies just now, we feel we are battling our fertility with pills or barriers as our weapons. Our hormones shift dramatically before our periods and make us crabby, weepy, or overly sensitive. We groan when we see blood in our underwear and grab something quickly to absorb it. Yet menstrual blood signals life, fertility, youth, and health. Our fertility and health is not something to fight against as an enemy or a disease, but to steward with wisdom and gratitude. Our bodies are sites of God's blessing and creative power.

In Mary's Magnificat I see deep gratitude and celebration for what God has done and will do in her body, though her suffering will increase as a result. Her coming shame is a reality she doesn't dwell on; she is focused on God's grace to her, on his mercy to her nation and to the world through Jesus. Her perspective is rightly placed; he is God, and she is his servant. And because she is seeing rightly, she is able to give herself to honest and heartfelt worship. She is in the story, but she is not the focus of it.

Jesus' choice to take on flesh tells us something else significant: Bodies are an important part of the human creature. When God created Adam and Eve, he did not merely cloak ethereal souls in skin and bones. He created bodies, the man from dust and the woman from the man, and breathed life into them. Jesus, to be fully human, took on a body with all its limits. He slept when his body got tired, he ate when his body was hungry, and he died when his body was killed. His body was raised from the dead, somehow transformed yet still human enough to eat, touch and be touched, and be both recognizable as Jesus and mistaken for a gardener. He ascended while still in possession of his body, which sits at the right hand of God.

Heresies throughout Christian history have derided the body in favor of the spirit. Gnosticism considered the body as something to be shed as one achieved higher spiritual knowledge. Extreme ascetics considered bodies shameful and less spiritual, and they often beat their bodies or denied them nourishment to make the soul stronger as the body was disciplined. Docetism falsely taught that Jesus only appeared human but was not fully so. God chose incarnation willingly and deliberately. Had the human problem been merely ignorance, as many religions teach, Jesus could have foregone the human experience and unsavory death and educated people through other means. But sin was the problem, and it enveloped every part of humanity. To defeat sin Jesus had to die a real death—which he could only achieve in a real body. Resurrection, too, could only happen to a *real* body. Bodies are clearly important to God, and they are part of what makes us human. While many people envision a disembodied eternity in heaven, the Bible teaches that at the resurrection we will receive transformed bodies that we will have forever. We are not just souls cloaked in dreadful bodies that we will someday escape. We are bodies, too.

When I told my grandma that I was pregnant the first time, she recalled her first pregnancy and how she had to stop working when she was five months pregnant, in rural Arkansas. I wondered aloud whether she had complications and was put on bed rest—many women work right up through the ninth month without any problems! She laughed, saying that once a woman in those days was visibly pregnant, she did not go out. Her new curves were a source of shame, a sign for all the public that she had had sex (though she was married!). Thankfully, pregnant roundness is more appreciated for its own special beauty these days. Although at other times we may feel cultural pressure to subject our bodies to strict diets to achieve thinness, in pregnancy we're free to revel in our curves and in our food. Pregnancy is an opportunity for us to enjoy our bodies and care for them well, appreciating God's design. It's an opportunity for us to ground ourselves fully in our bodies.

A better theology of the body is needed as a baseline when we consider the implications of childbirth for women and babies. How we view our bodies and evaluate the work being done during childbirth affects decisions that we make before, during, and after birth. Is the body conspiring against the woman with forces to be fought against and medicated into submission? Is the body doing good and hard work that the woman can be fully present in and help along? Is it some of both at times? Pregnancy grounds us in the goodness and wonder of our bodies, and it forces us to be in tune with our bodies as never before. There is no room for fanciful, disembodied spirituality in pregnancy. Our theology of the body has real-life implications for childbirth. In the next chapter, we'll explore injustices done to the bodies of mothers as they give birth as a result of a poor view of the body and birth. We'll also discover that the kingdom of God has come near to bring good news to those who face injustice and suffering, and the language to describe this kingdom is preached in the language of birth.

Spiritual Disciplines for Chapter 3

God's creation of childbirth, and his participation in it through the incarnation, redefines and imparts sacredness to birth. Jesus and Mary provide examples of trusting submission to God in birth, in life, and in death. Even in the midst of painful submission, we can have joyful celebration.

In this section, we will practice the disciplines of submission and celebration. As a focal passage, we'll use Philippians 2:1–11. Here we see the call to imitate Jesus in humble submission in our relationships with others (2:1–5); Jesus' submission to servanthood, humanity, and even death (2:6–8); and then the celebration of his exaltation (2:9–11). Mary's Magnificat (Luke 1:46–55) also gives us a poetic outburst of celebration in the midst of submission to God. Jesus and Mary both show us that in losing our lives, we will find them (Matt 10:39; Mark 8:35; Luke 9:24; 17:33; John 12:25). Pregnancy and childbirth provide us with an opportunity to engage in submission and celebration with intensity that few other stages of life do.

Submission

Submission is deliberately and willfully "giving in" to God and to others. Rather than passively taking life as it comes, submission is an active decision that considers the needs of others above ourselves, giving us freedom from our need to control and manipulate others into doing things our way. The discipline of submission allows us to release ourselves to God's care in full and complete trust. Our culture speaks of submission as an act of weakness. However, the Bible describes Jesus' submission to the limitations of an earthly body, his submission to God the Father in all things, and his willing submission to death. Jesus' incarnation turns the normal definition of power on its head. For the church, submission between spouses, slave and owner, and children and parents are all commanded, in the manner of Jesus. Mary's submission to God in bearing Jesus provides us with an excellent example as well. Submission begins in the heart with an attitude of humility and self-denial, and it overflows into our actions and words. Submission to God is, paradoxically, a sign of great strength!

We are always submitting ourselves to something—whether it is to our own selfish interests, fear, the opinions of others, anger, love, or truth. If we do not consciously practice submission to God and to others, we may believe that we are free people who give in to no one and nothing. The truth is, we are slaves to our own sin and will usually have a bent toward submission to our sinful nature. Those who practice the discipline of submission recognize that natural leaning toward sin and instead deliberately yield themselves to God.

There are many opportunities to practice submission in pregnancy—both submission to God and submission to something destructive. In becoming pregnant, we submit our bodies to all kinds of stresses and changes—weight gain, stretch marks, changed diets, morning sickness. We submit to these things because we love our babies and value their lives above our own comfort. We also have the opportunity to submit ourselves to selfishness, making poor prenatal decisions that increase risks for the baby. In childbirth, we're presented anew with the uncertainty of the future, and we can choose to submit our fears to God. We can also choose to submit to our fears. In labor, if we submit to contractions' good role in birthing the baby, rather than fighting contractions as the enemy, birth will be faster and easier. If things go wrong in childbirth, we can submit ourselves to God for healing rather than submitting ourselves to bitterness or guilt. We can accept that we could not control everything that happened and release ourselves from the terrible burden of perceived failure.

Submission to God's care and to the interests of others allows us to be controlled by love rather than fear in pregnancy and labor. Let me be clear: I am not advocating blind obedience to the demands of caregivers or hospital protocols to make birth attendants more comfortable or to be a good patient. Sometimes holding the interests of your child above your own may mean going against standardized hospital protocols or challenging (even changing) your caregiver. Sometimes it means submitting your birth plan and your hopes for your birth to the skilled medical staff and accepting this unexpected path with God's strength. Submitting even a traumatic birth to God is empowering, because it releases you from victimhood. When you couldn't choose anything else, you could choose to submit your life and health and child to God in trust. Submission is also the opposite of avoiding issues like difficult emotions that may come up. Avoidance runs away; submission leans in.

Celebration

Modern spirituality is full of cynicism, legalism, and sometimes one-upping each other in how much we have suffered for Jesus. At times, we simply feel weary from life. Perhaps worst of all is the general sense of apathy and indifference. These forces may pull us down into a mind-set that believes God is distant and uncaring, and further stress threatens to break our trust of him forever. By undertaking the discipline of celebration, we are actively moving ourselves toward God in gratitude and trust, and we find that he has been with us the whole time. Celebration acts as a powerful antidote to our Pharisaism and cynicism, and it energizes us for moving through life with God as we seek his love and faithfulness intentionally.

We celebrate not with some superficial, contrived joy. God has broken into our lives, into the mundane, into the misery, and he has redeemed it all. Richard Foster teaches, "When the power that is in Jesus reaches into our work and play and redeems them, there will be joy where once there was mourning. To overlook this is to miss the meaning of the Incarnation. ... Celebration comes when common ventures of life are redeemed."[13] Childbirth is a visible example of God reaching into our lives, redeeming what is there, and turning mourning into joy. Jesus even uses a mother's grief over labor and her joy over her child's birth as an example of his disciples' grief turning to joy at his resurrection (John 16:20–22). Celebration is most joyous following a difficult struggle.

Thus, the first step to celebration is acknowledging the ways that God has entered into our lives—the reason for celebration in the first place. Understanding his kindness, generosity, grace, knowledge of us, his greatness and his sacrifice on our behalf—these all lead to gratitude and celebration welling up in us.

Exercises for Submission and Celebration

1. Keep a daily journal of gifts that God has given you, big or small. The book *One Thousand Gifts* by Ann Voskamp is one resource that may be helpful if you are not convinced of the deep power of gratitude to overcome a hard heart.[14]

2. Find ways to honor and celebrate your pregnant or postpartum body. Retrain your thoughts and your words about your body, considering the ways your body has shown the creativity of God's work. Make a plan for taking better care of your body through good eating, exercise, rest, and self-care.

3. Write your own Magnificat, celebrating what God has done in your life as you have submitted yourself to him in trust. Or if you don't write, use the gifts God has given you—singing, painting, talking, dancing—the options are limitless! Use your gifts to celebrate childbirth and the rites of pregnancy and postpartum, for yourself and for others. Create celebratory rituals for certain milestones or write liturgy or prayers or hymns, honoring God's work in childbirth within the community of the church.

4. Write down your fears for pregnancy, labor, and/or postpartum. Write the heavy ones that break your heart to even consider and the silly fears you'd never admit to anyone (pooping on the delivery table is a common one!). Now look at them. If your future self experiences one of these, what would you tell her? Why would these things be difficult for you? What do you think will happen in your heart if these things happen? Do not dwell in despair over things that have not happened, but also do not let yourself believe they couldn't happen. Our fears scare us

because they *could* happen. Bring your fears to God one by one and ask for his peace to cover you—for the ability to trust his nearness and care for you in joy and in suffering.

5. If you are overwhelmed by fear and anxiety and have symptoms of panic—such as shortness of breath, tightness in your chest, a pounding or fluttering heart, and feelings of being overwhelmed—there are things you can do. Stop what you are doing and sit comfortably. Close your eyes and inhale deeply through your nose, counting to eight. Hold your breath for a few seconds, then release through your mouth in eight counts. Repeat this careful, controlled breathing as you pray something very simple, such as, "Help me, Jesus." Try to relax every muscle in your body, from your head to your toes, especially concentrating on places where you hold stress—back, shoulders, stomach, and fists. I find that holding my hands open, palms up in a releasing and receiving position, helps me to focus my prayers on my good Father who wants me to bring my troubles to him and receive grace in abundance. (This is great for labor or even Braxton-Hicks contractions. Relaxing the body stops that adrenaline from ramping up your pain and anxiety. As each contraction rises, focus intently on praying, releasing your fears and your muscles, and receiving God's grace. The less you fight the contractions, the more you will open up.)

6. Search out what Scripture says about fear. Choose a few passages you want to memorize, create art from, or write on an index card. Have your labor supporters remind you of these passages during labor, and actively submit your heart to the peace of God each time fear rises up. If you need help getting started, some of my favorite passages about fear are Isaiah 41:10–14; Philippians 4:6–7; and Psalm 91.

7. Consider various relationships in your life and examine the ways you submit yourself to the interests of others rather than to your own gain or ambition. Meditate on Philippians 2:1–14 and ask the Lord to show you how you can be free from the need to always have your own plans realized.

CHAPTER 4

New Birth into the Kingdom of God

Therefore, if anyone is in Christ, he is a new creation. The old has passed away; behold, the new has come.

—2 Corinthians 5:17 ESV

Holly's Story

Kris and I were elated to find out I was pregnant, and we told everyone the news that same day. I carefully thought through every detail of my birth plan and decided I'd try for an unmedicated birth in our local, small-town hospital. When labor began, Kris and I walked the neighborhood, relaxing and timing the contractions. I had no pain, just a little discomfort. I was so proud of myself—I wasn't feeling any pain even with contractions coming every four to five minutes. When my water broke, we headed to the hospital as the contractions intensified.

At the hospital, I began to feel like I was starting to lose control. I was put into a bed; when they checked my progress, I was already dilated to four centimeters. The contractions were quick and intense. Because of the late hour, many of the medical staff were going home. I was told upon arrival that the anesthesiologist would be leaving soon, so if I wanted an epidural I had better get it immediately. I didn't want one, but the pain was getting more intense, so I panicked. I had wanted to try the birthing tub, walk the halls, use a birthing ball—all the options I'd read about—but the questions and the stern manner of the nurses scared me. They pushed me for a fast answer, so out of fear, I consented. The pain did subside and I was able to get a little rest, but my labor also slowed to a halt. I stopped dilating for almost two hours.

When it was time to push, the epidural wore off and the pain became unbearable. They kept telling me the baby was coming, but that I wasn't pushing right and he couldn't get out. They had to use the suction cup [vacuum extractor] on his head, but it failed. I pushed for over two hours while they suctioned his head three different times. So they said the words I feared most: "emergency cesarean."

I went into the operating room panicking and crying. I lay there with a big blue tarp between me and the chaos. Many doctors and nurses entered the room, and I didn't understand why. I asked the anesthesiologist what was happening, and she lied, saying everything was fine. A woman's voice, not my doctor, was on the other side cussing. I looked to Kris, but he almost fainted. Everyone was talking and no one would tell me what was going on. Finally I heard a tiny sound, but only for a moment. My baby was here, and then maybe he wasn't.

I asked again what was going on, and I was told my baby wasn't breathing but everything would be okay. I lost it! I listened as hard as I could for another cry, and it never came. After six minutes of resuscitation, he finally let out a scream. He was alive! A nurse whisked him out of the room, his head full of fluid from the suction and his eye black from the trauma of his birth. I was sad not to be going with him and not sure why they had to take him so soon, but I figured they knew best and I would just have to wait. I was having major bleeding problems and had to remain in the operating room for quite a while.

The next month was a whirlwind. I had to have several blood transfusions after the section. Then I developed a massive bacterial infection around my uterus, which made my small intestine stop working. I stayed in the intensive care unit for three weeks with an NG tube down my throat and drains coming out of my belly. I could barely see my son, and I was terrified to hold him, thinking one of the bags attached to my many drains would open all over him. I thought I was dying, and I was nearly ready to give up.

When I finally did go home, I was consumed by all my medications, the care for my wound vacuums and drains, and trying to become a functional human again. My son, Anderlan, was diagnosed as a "failure to thrive," underweight with a poor suck reflex that made him burn more calories trying to eat than he could get from milk. I felt like the worst mother. Guilt, anger, and grief overwhelmed me for months. This was not the first year of motherhood I'd dreamed of for so long.

Holly's first childbirth was traumatic. Perhaps elements of her story remind you of your own birthing experience: fear, losing control, stern and pushy birth attendants, being put on a timer for labor, anger or guilt over the way things turned out. Perhaps you had a cesarean and felt the fear of what was going on behind the tarp. While these elements are common, the dramatic results of Holly's emergency cesarean are far more rare than movies might make them seem. But her story sheds light on the injustice present in our American maternity care system, which often pressures mothers into fitting into their system of carefully timed and unnecessarily medicated births. Many of us overlook what happened in the laboring room because of the beautiful baby in our arms. We may even blame ourselves if something goes wrong; we say we should have listened to the professionals better or done more research on this or that, or we should have just known by a mother's intuition.

When birth trauma happens, it may confirm our beliefs that childbirth is a curse on women, inherently dangerous, and a medical event rather than a sacred turn in our story. We may see childbirth as a punishment rather than as a means of grace that shapes our souls. Holly's story illuminates common problems in the American maternity system, opening a window into birth injustice found around the world. But Holly's story—as we'll see later—also illustrates how God can work in traumatic, unexpected turns in birth stories to shape women.

Birth Injustice and the Medical System

Little-known fact: The United States straggles behind almost 50 countries in maternal mortality rates—despite spending more money per capita on health care than any other country in the world.[1] However, there is no nationally funded requirement for hospitals to report medical errors and causes of death for mothers and babies, so these numbers are not entirely accurate. Because of the lack of reporting measures, the Centers for Disease Control and Prevention estimated in 1998 that maternal mortality rates were likely 1.3 to 3 times as high as reported.[2]

Many studies suggest that America's high-tech, overmedicated approach to labor and delivery has not made childbirth safer; on the contrary, these practices may lead to more interventions, complications, and even death. Ricki Lake's 2008 documentary *The Business of Being Born* opened the eyes of thousands to the realities, injustices, and politics of the modern American maternity system. The culmination of technology-driven birth, the bottom-line mentality of insurance companies, and pressure placed on hospitals and medical staff have created an increasingly unsafe environment for mothers and babies.

Women are not well informed of their options for their own bodies and babies, and they are often not educated or equipped to make important decisions on their own before labor. Rather than taking a proactive role in preparing for childbirth, many women sign over the decisions and responsibilities for their births to their doctors. In truth, few obstetricians in the United States are trained to handle normal, uneventful births; their medical residencies are spent in the operating theater, handling childbirth complications. Thus trained to look for complications, U.S. obstetricians may be quick to suggest surgical solutions for issues that have not historically warranted surgery, such as breech births, twin births, or a birth after a previous cesarean. In most countries with better birth outcomes, midwives remain the primary caregivers for low-risk pregnant women, only consulting obstetricians for complications that may arise. This model of maternal care assumes that birth is a normal process, rather than a medical event to be managed and treated.

In 2013, the U.S. rate of cesarean births was 32.7 percent of all births.[3] According to the World Health Organization (WHO), optimal and safe C-section rates for a country are about 10 to 15 percent.[4] Countries that fall below 10 percent usually have such insufficient access to medical care that more surgical care is needed to save the lives of mothers and babies. The WHO has warned the United States that its C-section rates are dangerously high for mothers and babies. While many claim that Americans have more complications in pregnancy than other countries and the rates cannot match WHO guidelines, San Francisco General Hospital managed a 10 percent rate of cesareans for first-time mothers in 2013,[5] using nurse-midwives for primary care, a salary-pay system for doctors rather than pay-per-surgery, and an abundance of evidence-based medical practices rather than the typical hospital protocols found in the United States.[6]

As soon as a laboring mother is admitted into a hospital in the United States, she is put on a clock. "Acceptable" progression (generally one centimeter of cervical dilation per hour) is allowed, but slower labors may be subject to artificial augmentation.[7] Many mothers no longer begin labor on their own but are induced for reasons ranging from a baby too large for vaginal delivery (though ultrasound estimates can be off by as much as a pound) to the passing of the due date (though normal birth generally occurs anywhere from 37 to 42 weeks' gestation—a span of five weeks!). Some women request induction, exhausted from pregnancy and eager to hold their babies. Sometimes inductions are scheduled around vacations or a doctor's busy schedule—birth is, after all, notoriously unpredictable and inconvenient. In the United States, the rate of induction of labor has increased from 9 percent in 1990 to 22.1 percent in 2004.[8] Inductions increase the risks of fetal distress from unnaturally long and hard contractions, increase the rate of cesareans, and may be the cause of respiratory issues in babies who needed to gestate longer.[9] For some women, the benefits of induction outweigh the risks—in cases of preeclampsia, fetal distress, or other medical conditions that may call for an immediate delivery, induction may be a brilliant alternative to a cesarean. But for healthy mothers and babies, the risks involved are not often worth taking.

Electronic fetal monitoring is used in nearly every hospital birth in the United States, requiring mothers to sit still, strapped to a bed, often in a reclining position to get the best reading of contractions and the baby's heart rate. Reclining is likely to cause more pain, putting increased pressure on the mother's back and pelvis. With her feet up in stirrups for pushing and delivery, the mother's position is advantageous for medical attendants but quite poor for the mother. A better position would be one that uses gravity and movement and takes pressure off the mother's back, such as squatting, sitting upright, or even standing.[10]

A woman is told to avoid all drugs if possible during pregnancy to protect her baby, yet in labor she is given all manner of drugs to control pain and augment labor. It is not well known among laboring mothers that epidurals commonly slow down labor or that narcotics can negatively impact the baby's breathing after birth. More synthetic oxytocin is often needed to speed labor back up, which requires an increased epidural dosage to manage the pain of the augmented contractions. This cycle often accelerates until a baby is distressed, and the mother is whisked off to the operating theater. Epidurals also increase the need for instrumental deliveries by forceps or vacuum extraction, which increase risk of injury to mother and baby.

Most mothers are generally unaware of the possible dangers of these interventions, which, in healthy mothers and babies, are often unnecessary. They often spiral into a cascade of interventions until a cesarean is needed. While cesareans are common, they are not risk free. A cesarean is a major abdominal surgery, with a long, painful recovery required afterward—while the mother also cares for a newborn! Risks include blood clots, reactions to anesthesia, increased bleeding, infections, and an increased risk of complication in subsequent pregnancies, such as placenta problems or uterine rupture. Babies born by C-section have much higher rates of respiratory issues and can also risk injury in the surgery. No doubt about it, cesareans can save lives! But such high intervention and C-section rates pose increased dangers to mothers and babies when they are not necessary, exposing them to trauma that could be avoided. Many birth professionals promote evidence-based care for women in pregnancy, childbirth, and postpartum. Unfortunately, birth practices prevalent in many hospitals in the United States and around the world are based not on scientifically backed research, but on traditions that go against evidence, nature, and, sometimes, common sense. Increased use of evidence-based practices can reduce pain, anxiety, trauma, and even death in childbirth.

There are many injustices at play in our complicated maternity system. Insurance companies fight against a culture overeager to sue doctors and hospitals, which often resort to cesareans to say they did everything possible for the mother and baby. The reliance on technology takes human intuition and personal monitoring away from the birthing process. The underlying culture of fear surrounding childbirth in the West feeds into all of this, nurturing a system that makes birth more dangerous for mothers and babies alike.

Racial injustice continues to plague the United States in birth as in other areas of life. According to the Center for Disease Control and Prevention, infant mortality among African-Americans is twice that among Caucasian babies.[11] Factors that play into these statistics are complicated and multifaceted, but they are worth untangling for the safety of all mothers and babies. The greatest birth injustices, however, are among the poor in our world—a problem not confined to the United States. The World Health Organization states:

> Every day, approximately 800 women die from preventable causes related to pregnancy and childbirth. 99% of all maternal deaths occur in developing countries. More than half of these deaths occur in sub-Saharan Africa and almost one third occur in South Asia. Maternal mortality is higher in women living in rural areas and among poorer communities.[12]

Further studies found that main causes of death among these women were bleeding, infections following childbirth, obstruction (often from poorly formed pelvic bones caused by malnutrition), and undetected preeclampsia. The simplest of skilled medical care could prevent many of these deaths. Other causes of death were diseases like AIDS and malaria as well as failed abortions. Many young girls are married off to men in areas wracked by poverty, and they get pregnant before their bodies are fully developed, making birth more dangerous. Roots of many of these deaths are poverty, lack of education, and lack of access to basic medical care.

Where I live in the Middle East, women are often kept in the dark concerning their own health care, even as they birth child after child. When my friend Sarah visited Fatima[13] in the hospital after the birth of her ninth child, Fatima shoved a stack of medical records in Sarah's hands to give to the doctor. Fatima, who is illiterate, had no idea that her records showed multiple treatments for sexually transmitted diseases given to her by her unfaithful husband. As a result of her many back-to-back pregnancies, her uterus was also prolapsed, hanging into her cervix, giving her great pain. No doctor had explained her medical conditions or warned her not to become pregnant again. Sons are highly prized; she will likely bear as many children as she can. Fatima's life is in very great danger from the marital and medical injustices done to her.

Cultural injustices also affect women during childbirth. In many parts of North Africa and the Middle East, female circumcision, or female genital mutilation (FGM), is a common cultural practice, affecting about 200 million girls and women worldwide. In FGM, some or all of the external genital tissue is removed, often as a way of controlling female sexual desires, which are seen as a danger to the community. It is frequently done with an unsterilized razor or a knife, and in most cases is performed between infancy and adolescence.[14] Women who have had FGM face significantly more danger in childbirth than those who haven't. The risks of hemorrhage, obstruction, and the death of either mother or baby are significantly higher among these women.

Childbirth is surrounded by injustice globally in various forms. We might be tempted to downplay the injustices in wealthier countries, because we "don't have it as bad as developing nations." Their plight is overwhelming, indeed. But God's heart is not merely for less brokenness—he desires wholeness, peace, and justice for *all* mothers and babies worldwide. He desires for his will to be done on earth as it is in heaven. He desires for his kingdom to come.

The Kingdom of God

Jesus came preaching one main message: "The kingdom of God has come near" (see Mark 1:15; Matt 3:2; and related passages). What exactly *is* the kingdom of God? If this was Jesus' primary message, we need to have a good grasp on what he was conveying. Preachers and teachers often explain the kingdom of God as another name for heaven—by which they mean a place up in the clouds where disembodied souls live behind pearly gates and streets of gold. But is this truly Jesus' message in the Bible?

We learned in the previous chapter that bodies are important to God. He created them as good, he inhabits a body as the incarnate Jesus Christ, and he plans to resurrect our bodies and transform them to be like his own body in the age to come. Bodies are not throwaways. Jesus' ministry was remarkably physical as well as spiritual, emotional, and mental. Because he created whole humans, God sought to restore whole humans—not just their souls. Jesus' incarnation, his embodiment in the same flesh as the rest of humanity, began redeeming what was broken. His restoration of bodies was a sign that the kingdom of God was active in the world. The lame walked. The blind could see. The dead were raised. The sick were healed. The hungry were fed.

But of course, Jesus didn't stop there. He lifted the heads of the shamed. He gathered in the outcasts and ate with them. He touched those who hadn't been touched in years because of their uncleanness. In this way, Jesus sought the wholeness of their hearts and emotions. He didn't divide humans into souls and bodies, or his ministry into our typical "evangelism" or "social justice" categories. His ministry was holistic—for the entire human. He cast out demons. He spoke, and the wind and waves obeyed him. Jesus has authority and power over the spiritual realms, over nature, and over the entire earth. He has power over death itself through his resurrection. This is the King of the cosmos, the Lord of both the spiritual and physical realms.

Before he ascended, Jesus gave a commission to his followers: Go and tell the good news to everyone. "Good news" was a common phrase in the Roman Empire. While this "good news" could be used in a variety of ways, Jesus was likely investing the word with new meaning in the context of the rule of the Roman emperors. In the days before social media, an emperor's inauguration would be announced by a proclaimer who would go out among the people and pronounce the *euangelion*—the "good news" or "glad tidings." He might also announce the good news if his king had won a battle or war: The king is victorious!

Jesus' kingdom has been announced; the *true* King is here. His kingdom broke into this world with Jesus' birth, life, death, and resurrection. We can experience the kingdom in many ways— through healings and answered prayers, through God's presence to us through the Holy Spirit actively working in us, in communities that take care and nurture one another by the power of God, in those who turn from sin and death to walk with God in life and holiness. When broken people find wholeness, then the kingdom of God has come near. We find wholeness when our lives are enveloped in the life of God.

The kingdom is here already—but it hasn't yet come in fullness. We long for the day when we won't grieve the death of loved ones. We wait for the day when our bodies won't get sick or old, when we won't feel the stab of betrayal, when we won't question God's nearness because we will see him face-to-face. Jesus taught us to pray for his kingdom to come, where God's will is done on earth as it is in heaven. God's will is for peace, justice, righteousness, and wholeness—for us, and for all of creation. Until his kingdom comes in fullness, we wait and we pray for it to come. Until Jesus returns, our job is this: proclaim that he is King to the whole world, enjoining them to find life in this kingdom by bowing down to King Jesus.

In Matthew 10, Jesus sends the twelve disciples out among Israel, saying, "Go rather to the lost sheep of Israel. As you go, proclaim this message: 'The kingdom of heaven has come near.' Heal the sick, raise the dead, cleanse those who have leprosy, drive out demons" (10:6–8). In other words, they were to do what Jesus himself was doing. He is our Savior and our example, and what's more, he sent the Holy Spirit so that we could be empowered to bear witness to the living Jesus and to proclaim the good news in word and in deed.

Childbirth and Kingdom People

So what does all of this have to do with giving birth? As we wait for God's kingdom to come, we are to also be active participants in its work, as those united with Christ, doing God's will on earth as it is done in heaven in the power of the Holy Spirit. We seek justice for the weak and the marginalized, as God does throughout Scripture. We become the voices for the traumatized, the weary, the refugee. We declare that Jesus is King over the entire cosmos and that he reigns over and cares for pregnant mothers and their babies. We pray and work for justice for mothers and babies around the world, that God's will may be done on earth as it is in heaven. We alleviate suffering in the name of Jesus, giving food to the hungry and bringing healing to the sick, lifting the heads of the shamed. We don't do this because we can make the world perfect—the world groans in labor and awaits new birth (Rom 8:22). We do this because we love God, and when we are close to his heart, we find our neighbors—near and far—there, too. We do this to proclaim the victory of an upside-down kingdom that calls the poor in spirit, the mourning, and the hungry blessed. We do this to follow our slaughtered Lamb-turned-Lion in the way of sacrificial love, because he says that we will find life even as we lay our lives down.

We should try in the ways we can, with the wisdom God gives, to bring wholeness and justice in the delivery rooms and labor huts. The injustices found in birth practices the world over are overwhelming. But don't fall for all-or-nothing excuses that say if you can't fix all the problems, then you might as well do nothing. We *can* work to improve birth as a sign of God's coming reign as it breaks into our world. We can listen to God and say "yes" to him in our own corners of the world rather than shrugging off hard work because the task seems too large and impossible. As kingdom people, we seek wholeness for our neighbors, whoever they might be.

Can childbirth proclaim the kingdom of God? Can you have a labor where you are loved and given dignity, not shame? Can you find peace and stillness and grace in the midst of the waves? Can the new life you bring forth from your body be a sign of hope and restoration and newness? The biblical writers may have thought so. Through metaphors, they often linked childbirth and the kingdom of God.

Birth as Entry into the Kingdom

Especially in the writings of John, birth is used as a metaphor for entry into the kingdom of God. Most of us are familiar with the phrase "born-again Christian"— though it sometimes sounds backwards and Bible-thumping to younger, more progressive ears.

Poor usage, though, doesn't make it unbiblical. Let's explore the richness of this phrase.

> Now there was a Pharisee, a man named Nicodemus who was a member of the Jewish ruling council. He came to Jesus at night and said, "Rabbi, we know that you are a teacher who has come from God. For no one could perform the signs you are doing if God were not with him."
> Jesus replied, "Very truly I tell you, no one can see the kingdom of God unless they are born again."
> "How can someone be born when they are old?" Nicodemus asked. "Surely they cannot enter a second time into their mother's womb to be born!"
> Jesus answered, "Very truly I tell you, no one can enter the kingdom of God unless they are born of water and the Spirit. Flesh gives birth to flesh, but the Spirit gives birth to spirit. You should not be surprised at my saying, 'You must be born again.' The wind blows wherever it pleases. You hear its sound, but you cannot tell where it comes from or where it is going. So it is with everyone born of the Spirit" (John 3:1–8).

A Pharisee comes to Jesus, and Jesus confronts his law-following salvation with radical words three times: Unless one is "born again" or "born of the Spirit," they cannot see the kingdom of God (John 3:3, 5, 7). As New Testament scholar Leon Morris writes, "Nicodemus and all his tribe of law-doers are left with not the slightest doubt but that what is asked of anyone is not more law, but the power of God within that person to remake him or her completely."[15] Here the word translated "again" could also easily be "above," so perhaps Nicodemus was asking for clarification between "born again" and "born from above."[16] Jesus seems to merge the two concepts rather than distinguish them—people need rebirth that can only come from God. As stated in the previous chapter, Jesus' conception by the Holy Spirit paved the way for us to be born from above in the power of the Holy Spirit too.

The description of being born "of water and the Spirit" (3:5) is a difficult combination to understand. Many assume "water" to symbolize baptism, but Jesus had not instituted baptism as a rite of initiation among his followers. Physical birth was sometimes described in terms of "birth by water," referencing the amniotic fluid. Thus, "born by water and by Spirit" might symbolize first a physical birth, and a second, spiritual rebirth. However, Jesus is likely proclaiming an Old Testament prophetic message that Nicodemus would have been familiar with as a Pharisee. "Water" and "Spirit" go together in several prophetic passages promising renewal and redemption during an era when God would pour out his Spirit on all people. Gary Burge notes that in these passages, "'Water and Spirit' are easily joined as the life-giving gifts of God."[17] Even in passages where water isn't explicitly mentioned, the image of "pouring" out the Spirit suggests water and renewal:

> For I will *pour water* on the thirsty land,
>   and *streams* on the dry ground;
> I will *pour out* my *Spirit* on your offspring,
>   and my blessing on your descendants (Isa 44:3).

> I will *pour out* my *Spirit* on all people.
> Your sons and daughters will prophesy,
>   your old men will dream dreams,
>   your young men will see visions.
> Even on my servants, both men and women,
>   I will *pour out* my *Spirit* in those days (Joel 2:28–29).

> I will sprinkle clean *water* on you, and you will be clean;
> I will cleanse you from all your impurities and from all
> your idols. I will give you a new heart and put a new
> *spirit* in you; I will remove from you your heart of stone
> and give you a heart of flesh. And I will put my *Spirit* in
> you and move you to follow my decrees and be careful
> to keep my laws (Ezek 36:25–27).

Jesus was proclaiming a regeneration available only by the power of God—one that was promised and is fulfilled in Christ.

He himself is the water promised by the prophets; he is the one who would bless, satiate thirst, cleanse, and restore (John 4:1–14). Birth is a brilliant metaphor for this regeneration in the lives of those who encounter Jesus. In birth, a human emerges in new life through "water." The baby has done nothing to be born; he was conceived by his parents, was formed and nourished in the womb of another person, and is brought into the world by the hard work of his mother. At birth, expectation and yearning and waiting burst forth into wails of new life. A transformation occurs— the squirmy ball within the mother, jabbing her ribs and rolling around, is now a separate entity, a child with her own story ahead of her. And while this child is separate from her parents as her own person, she bears resemblance to her parents in many ways. These resemblances often increase as the child grows, adapting mannerisms and behaviors of her parents as well as the physical features she shares with them.

In the context of regeneration, being "born of the Spirit" or "born again" is certainly a miraculous and awe-worthy image. God takes a person with sin and smudges, with a heart of stone that cannot will enough goodness and holiness to please him, and he gives them a new birth. Suddenly this person is transformed in an unexplainable kind of newness, with a new heart open to God and full of his Spirit, with a new story ahead of him. This person begins to resemble God his Parent more and more as he is transformed into the image of God's Son (Rom 8:29). What did this person do to effect his birth? Just as much as a baby does. It is the power of God that brings life to people. And birth is the perfect metaphor to remind us of his life-giving, transformative, gospel power. Also drawing on the language of the prophets, Titus writes, "But when the kindness and love of God our Savior appeared, he saved us, not because of righteous things we had done, but because of his mercy. He saved us through the *washing of rebirth* and *renewal by the Holy Spirit*, whom he *poured out* on us generously through Jesus Christ our Savior" (Titus 3:4–6).

First John repeatedly describes those "born of God," depicting this radical renewal and transformation.[18] Several times, John declares that those born of God have certain characteristics as transformed people. Those who are born of God act in ways that display God's own love, character, and holiness. "No one who is *born of God* will continue to sin, because God's seed remains in them; they cannot go on sinning, because they have been *born of God.* This is how we know who the children of God are and who the children of the devil are: Anyone who does not do what is right is not God's child, nor is anyone who does not love their brother and sister" (1 John 3:9–10). Love is a birthmark of God's children: "Dear friends, let us love one another, for love comes from God. Everyone who loves has been *born of God* and knows God. Whoever does not love does not know God, because God is love" (4:7–8).

As if the rebirth of humans weren't enough, all of creation will experience this future rebirth. God is not only planning to set things right among people, but he will restore all he has made—the entire cosmos (Matt 19:28; Mark 9:12; Acts 3:21). Brenda B. Colijn writes, "The Spirit's renewal of individual lives is a foretaste of the future cosmic renewal. According to James 1:18, regenerated believers are the 'first fruits' of the renewal of creation."[19] Paul writes:

> The creation waits in eager expectation for the children of God to be revealed. For the creation was subjected to frustration, not by its own choice, but by the will of the one who subjected it, in hope that the creation itself will be liberated from its bondage to decay and brought into the freedom and glory of the children of God.
>
> We know that the whole creation has been groaning as in the pains of childbirth right up to the present time. Not only so, but we ourselves, who have the firstfruits of the Spirit, groan inwardly as we wait eagerly for our adoption to sonship, the redemption of our bodies (Rom 8:19–23).

The whole creation is in travail until the kingdom comes and new creation is birthed from the old.

This kingdom comes like labor: suddenly and unexpectedly. A "due date" is the most ridiculous misnomer ever created for pregnancy. As mentioned previously, a woman can go into labor any day between 37 and 42 weeks' gestation, and it is considered completely normal and healthy. Setting a particular day based on menstrual cycle patterns, which often vary widely from woman to woman, can be wildly inaccurate. Each woman's body and baby gestate uniquely, not in a standardized or robotic manner. The specific day of birth is nearly impossible to predict. Jesus told his disciples:

> For many will come in my name, claiming, "I am the Messiah," and will deceive many. You will hear of wars and rumors of wars, but see to it that you are not alarmed. Such things must happen, but the end is still to come. Nation will rise against nation, and kingdom against kingdom. There will be famines and earthquakes in various places. *All these are the beginning of birth pains.*
>
> Then you will be handed over to be persecuted and put to death, and you will be hated by all nations because of me. At that time many will turn away from the faith and will betray and hate each other, and many false prophets will appear and deceive many people. Because of the increase of wickedness, the love of most will grow cold, but the one who stands firm to the end will be saved. And this gospel of the kingdom will be preached in the whole world as a testimony to all nations, and then the end will come (Matt 24:5–14).

When Jesus returns with the fullness of the kingdom in his wake, there will be astonishment, pain, and trembling—but no one knows his due date.

Childbirth and Crisis

The Old Testament prophets used the aspect of uncertainty in childbirth as a metaphor for an impending crisis. Birth is generally a physiological process and not a pathological one—a normal part of life rather than a medical crisis. But for some women, birth may seem like a crisis or even become a true crisis. When women have poor access to health care, preventative care, good nutrition, or education, childbirth is more dangerous. It is in this world of danger and crisis that ancient Israelite women gave birth. As a result, the imagery of childbirth is often used to describe the emotions and physical reactions of people in crisis—particularly the crisis of facing God's judgment.

In Scripture, there is surprisingly little detail about the birth practices of ancient Israel. In Egypt, the Hebrew slaves were apparently attended by skilled Hebrew midwives (Exod 1:15-21). This passage mentions "the delivery stool" (1:16). In many Mesopotamian cultures and in ancient Egypt, women gave birth on low stools or while crouching on their hands and knees on piles of stacked bricks.[20]

Life was harsh during these times. As desert nomads for much of their history, ancient Israelites often experienced famine and lack of water. There was no prenatal testing or preventative care, and no cesareans that might have saved both mother and baby. It is likely that Rachel died giving birth to Benjamin because of a complicated breech birth—the midwife attending tried to comfort her before the birth was over that she was having a son (Gen 35:16-19). Further, the constant tribal warfare, centuries of slavery to Egypt, the wars of the conquest, the exiles to Assyria and Babylonia—these were quite violent times. Childbirth was significantly more dangerous for ancient Israelite women than it is for Western women today who have access to food, education, shelter, and peaceful political contexts. The prophetic writers used childbirth as a metaphor for crisis within a culture in which it was more common to face life or death in childbirth.

The physical reactions of women in labor are reinterpreted in passages of impending judgment, and they are applied to men to surprising and effective result. For instance, upon hearing bad news of coming enemies, men are found writhing in agony, groaning like a woman in childbirth, seized by terror, gripped by pain, trembling, bewildered or having a faltering heart, gasping, and panting (Psa 48:5-7; Isa 13:7-8; 21:2-4; 26:17-18; Jer 4:19, 31; 6:24; 13:21; 22:23; 30:4-6; 48:41-42; 49:20-24; Hos 13:12-14; Mic 4:9-10). These passages convey the emotions of anguish, terror, being out of control, and surprise that the onset of labor can bring. Once labor has begun, it is an unstoppable force. In most passages, a baby isn't mentioned—and this is the most agonizing picture of labor, one without hope of new life on the other side. Several passages describe these birth pangs as producing only wind, a baby that does not have the sense to emerge, or of laboring so hard that there is no strength left to deliver (2 Kgs 19:3; Isa 26:18; 37:3; Hos 13:13). What a picture of torture and agony! This is what awaits those who have long said yes to their sin and will not return to God.

Most passages using childbirth as a metaphor for crisis seem to leave us on a cliff-hanger between labor and birth: Will Israel be brought to new life? Will God pull them through the judgment he inflicts for their sins, or will he walk away from them? In some of these prophetic passages, however, God uses the crisis of childbirth to depict the painful struggle—with the expectation of hope and new life. Micah tells "Daughter Zion" to "writhe in agony ... like a woman in labor" as she is exiled in Babylon. But he continues, "There you will be rescued. There the LORD will redeem you out of the hand of your enemies" (Mic 4:9-10). In Isaiah 26, Israel says they "gave birth to wind" (26:18), but this is followed with the proclamation, "But your dead will live, LORD; their bodies will rise—let those who dwell in the dust wake up and shout for joy ... the earth will give birth to her dead" (26:19). God himself is depicted as a woman in labor, crying out and gasping and panting, to bring new life and light to those in darkness (Isa 42:14-16).

As we have seen in Jesus, new birth is coming. We are no longer on the edge of our seats, wondering whether God will rescue his people—he sent his own Son to be born so that we might be born of God. The story of Scripture is like a woman in labor—groaning, grunting, wailing, and wondering—and then the Redeemer emerges, bringing those who were in darkness into the light.

The gospel tells us the end of the story: New birth is here, and new birth is coming in full!

Grace in Birth

Holly experienced the emotions of this life-or-death crisis in a traumatic childbirth, but she was not left in hopelessness. She continues her story:

> In the months after Anderlan's birth, I was able to muster a smile and polite small talk, but inside I was hollow. I was despairing and missing all the good and miraculous around me. These feelings lasted about five months. My body was healing, but I never dealt with all the pain and loss of my childbirth experience.
>
> One day as I was reading my Bible and holding Anderlan, I was jolted into reality. As I was reading, I heard a voice deep within me say, "Who do you think you are?" It wasn't said in a sarcastic way, but more as a stern discipline. I sat there, wondering what it meant and if it had actually happened. As I continued in silence, I realized that it was clearly God speaking his words. Through this whole ordeal I had forgotten I was his. God was not trying to hurt me but was wanting to use my story to bring me into a closer communion with him and give him glory. I had forgotten who my Father was and that he works for the good of all who love and obey him. I then understood how my sins of selfishness and control for years had hindered and almost destroyed my relationship with him. I could finally see his hand in each moment, and joy and thankfulness swept over me. For truly the first time, I was able to look at Anderlan as a blessing and privilege rather than an event that happened. I saw a glimpse of how God works and his merciful care and purpose in everything.
>
> Giving birth ended up being a blessing in more ways than I could fathom. It brought a beautiful baby boy

into our lives. It showed me that God is sovereign and knows what we need when we need it most. And it brought everything back into perspective—glory is to God alone, and his purpose truly is best. His purpose alone should be sought after by his children in every area of their lives!

Even when our births take unexpected and perhaps traumatic turns, we belong to God, who turns our hardest stories down paths of surprising grace. God revealed to Holly exactly where he had been in her nightmare—right with her. Even bad childbirth experiences can be redeemed by God to turn us from sin and toward him. Isn't this the message of the gospel? God binds up the brokenhearted, sets captives free, and sets them within a new story—his.

Throughout the millennia, childbirth has been derided as a curse on women, a horror to be feared and faced until you can get past it to get to the baby on the other side. But in Scripture, birth is given dignity as a metaphor of transformation, of new life in Christ, and being reborn as a child of God. And our new birth serves as a signpost of an even more incredible one to come—when the entire cosmos is made new, birthed from the old. The entire process of childbirth is so profound, so miraculous, so incredible, that it requires worship of the One who created it. From his providence over conception to the knitting together of parts in the womb, from the widening of the cervix and vagina and the careful twisting of a body through the pelvic opening to the emergence of a brand-new life not manufactured, or sculpted, but *created,* God's work in childbirth is unbelievable. It should cause us to weep, as mothers often do when they feel the weight of the miracle, naked in their arms.

Who could have imagined that childbirth and worship could be so inextricably linked? Through childbirth, we better understand our birth into the kingdom of God, as needy newborns brought into light by the power and sweat and suffering of God. The gospel is proclaimed in childbirth if we have eyes to see and ears to hear. The convergence of childbirth and the kingdom of God should propel us into seeking justice in childbirth for women globally.

This convergence should show up in our art, in our liturgy and worship, in our medical practices, and in our discussions with our growing daughters, who may one day be mothers.

Our new birth was not achieved apart from the anguished labor of Jesus, who has given us new birth into this kingdom. In the next chapter, we will explore our connections with the suffering, death, and resurrection of Jesus as we ourselves endure pain for the sake of bringing another life.

Spiritual Disciplines for Chapter 4

In chapter 4, we discovered how biblical writers used the language of childbirth to describe entrance into God's kingdom, bringing a person into a new realm of life, hope, and newness. As members of this kingdom, we seek God's *shalom* as we await the day when creation itself is born anew. The metaphor of childbirth is also used in the Bible as an image of crisis for those who need to return to God and find restoration with him. Childbirth acts as a signpost that directs us back to our creator and the gospel of Jesus Christ.

In this section, we'll engage with the disciplines of proclaiming the gospel, confession, and forgiveness. These disciplines are intended to provide the opportunity for us to recognize where we have walked away from God in sin and allow the truth of his gospel of grace to draw us back to him in full reconciliation. Women who are pregnant and who deliver babies provide the church with a physical reminder of the gospel when taken with the teachings of Scripture outlined in chapter 4. The whole church benefits from watching its pregnant members in this stage of life.

Proclaiming the Gospel

When we join our life to Christ's, we are reborn by God as new creations, and we experience a life of freedom and wholeness under God's rule. Childbirth gives us a vivid image of this regeneration: A baby is born by the work of the mother, he is brought from darkness to light by her suffering, he undergoes a transformation from womb to world, and he is born into a future with his parents, whom he will imitate as he grows. When we give birth, we proclaim this gospel! God has programmed it into the common life so that we would see him in it. The discipline of proclaiming the gospel—to yourself and to others—is one that may come naturally or not. Childbirth gives us an incredible way to do this. The parallels of childbirth and regeneration are so natural that anyone can use this analogy to understand the gospel or explain it to others. It's a major reason I became a childbirth educator!

Jesus proclaimed that his kingdom was near and then used various signs as proof: the dead raised, the sick healed, demons cast out, the natural world obeying his word, the shamed restored, and sins forgiven. Where Jesus is King, *shalom* has been restored. In childbirth, we preach the gospel by seeking this *shalom* for mothers in whatever ways we can. We work for justice where there is injustice, we bring the peace and healing of Christ where there is chaos and trauma, and we proclaim grace where sin and guilt take hold. The discipline of preaching the gospel allows us to live beneath the cross, viewing our lives in the shadow of what Jesus has done.

Mothers who preach the gospel to themselves understand that they are sinners in desperate need of grace. They acknowledge their fears, sins, and weaknesses, knowing that they do not have to hide them—Jesus paid for them already. These mothers also move away from judgments against other mothers in their birth and mothering choices because they recognize that no one is perfect; all of us need the grace and wisdom of Jesus as we walk the difficult road of parenting. The gospel frees us from the need for approval or to earn God's favor by performing in a certain way. In childbirth, there is now no condemnation for any mother who chooses to be induced, gets an epidural, elects for a cesarean, or follows a poor birth plan. There is no extra credit for mothers who eat and exercise flawlessly during pregnancy or labor without any drugs. We are loved, accepted, and cherished by God in all the ways we give birth.

We also don't have to drum up the words for a "spiritual" child-birth if that's not the experience we had. We live in a world marred by sin; sometimes emergencies happen or the atmosphere is wrong or the hormones take over and we yell things we would never say under normal circumstances. But God's kingdom has also broken in, and sometimes we can experience births that are unexpectedly healing, peaceful, or even painless. Our birth is allowed to be what it is, because it joins with God's story of redemption. No matter how a birth may turn out, we can find Jesus there. Sometimes it is a matter of laying our story before him and asking him to show us where he was.

The gospel gives meaning and perspective to our birth stories. We are planted within the long narrative that began in Eden. We grieve as Eve sins and becomes an enemy of God, we listen as God promises hope through the birth of the One who would crush the serpent's head, we rejoice with angels and shepherds when Mary births the Son of God. This is our story. We cocreate with God as beloved colaborers; we bring new life into the world that images the transformative work God does in those who turn to him. We wait and groan with creation until the new cosmos is finally birthed. When we give birth, we proclaim this gospel, this story.

Confession and Forgiveness

Tied up with the gospel are the twin disciplines of confession and forgiveness. Most moms struggle with guilt, often over things they couldn't control. An unexpected birth experience, a past abortion, a difficult postpartum, a poor choice made during pregnancy, poor parenting choices—guilt is often a staple emotion for moms, and it only gets worse as we parent imperfectly. It is difficult to resolve guilt if we play the victim and fail to own any responsibility. We might truly be the victim if we did nothing wrong, but we find we cannot get past the event because of shame that isn't ours to own.

In my house, we frequently use the phrase, "Own your own stuff!" It is important that we own what we are responsible for, repent without justifying our sin, and release the rest that wasn't ours. If you were at fault, you have forgiveness ready to be lavished upon you by a merciful God—and if you were wronged, forgiveness may be the only way you are able to let go of your anger and hurt. In many circumstances, you may need both to confess and to forgive.

Confession is difficult. It forces us to be open and honest before God about all the things we likely hate most about ourselves.

James writes, "Confess your sins to each other and pray for each other so that you may be healed" (5:16). Couldn't we just confess to God and leave other people out of it? We could—Jesus is our only mediator before God (1 Tim 2:5). However, there is healing in laying ourselves open before a trustworthy person, confessing what we have done, and receiving grace and the pronouncement of forgiveness by God from someone's mouth. Speaking what we have done in the dark and bringing light into those shadows breaks the chains these sins had around us. It also gives another person the opportunity to proclaim the good news to us, and perhaps will give them the freedom to confess and be free of sin before you. Confession moves us into humility before God and others, removing the mask of self-righteousness and hypocrisy we are so prone to wear. Dealing properly with guilt is important for parenting little sinners! You are not only becoming a trustworthy parent, but you are also modeling apologizing and living a life before God that is open, authentic, and humble. You also have a wonderful opportunity in these moments to proclaim the gospel to your children.

When we forgive others, we do so in the way of God: *not* sweeping sin under the rug, pretending it didn't happen, or saying it wasn't so bad. We deal with it by naming our hurt and anger and sins and moving past them into new life. We restore broken relationships as we follow Jesus, who reconciled us to God. We are able to forgive because we know we have been forgiven. We are no longer slaves to bitterness, anger, grudges, or manipulation by others. We are free to forgive those who have not confessed their sins to us, and we are free to forgive those who are not even sorry they've hurt us. Sometimes it is appropriate to tell the offender you've forgiven them; sometimes it is not. Wise counsel and prayer can help in the discernment.

Exercises for Proclaiming the Gospel, Confession, and Forgiveness

1. Write down all the ways that childbirth is similar to what happens to a person when he or she comes to God in faith. Use biblical references where you can—the books of John and 1 John

are especially full of this language. Meditate on the ways that childbirth proclaims the gospel.

2. If you fear childbirth, ask for the peace passing understanding that Jesus gives—he came to bring *shalom*. If you are racked with guilt over choices you made, proclaim the gospel to yourself. If you are angry or hurt, preach the gospel to yourself.

3. Look for an opportunity to proclaim the gospel to one other person. Can you use the imagery of childbirth as the biblical writers do—to convey the total life transformation that Jesus brings? Can you explain the kingdom of God? How does the inauguration of the kingdom of God to this earth affect how you view birth, other mothers, or maternity-care injustices? How will you participate in this kingdom now that you are a citizen of it?

Use the following exercises for any sins you need to confess and sins others have committed against you, whether before pregnancy, during the birth, postpartum, or any other time in your life:

4. Write out the story of what happened. What were you feeling? What were the circumstances that led to it? Who else was to blame? List your specific sins: pride, laziness, out-of-control anger, poor communication, etc. What was done to you that was wrong? Be specific.

5. Say aloud what you have done to God. Confess your sins and repent of them. Consider ways you can submit yourself to him to curb long-standing sins. If you need to ask for someone's forgiveness and it is appropriate, go to that person, look him or her in the eye, and confess that what you did was wrong without trying to justify it. Say that you are truly sorry and would like to seek his or her forgiveness.

6. Say aloud what was done to you and admit that it was wrong. Ask God to forgive that person, and ask for his help so that you can forgive that person. How does the gospel of the kingdom of God fit into this situation?

CHAPTER 5

Pain, Suffering, and Resurrection in Childbirth

There are two extremes to avoid: being completely absorbed in your pain and being distracted by so many things that you stay far away from the wound you want to heal.

—Henri Nouwen, *The Inner Voice of Love*[1]

The Problem of Pain

When I arrived at the hospital in early labor with my first child, I presented a basic birth plan to the attending nurse: no pain medication, please. I had been sensitive to many medications in the past, and I had no desire to test out new drugs while giving birth to my son. However, there were other reasons I wanted to avoid pain relief, though I had never articulated them. I wanted to be a superior mother. I wanted to be someone who could handle "the most painful thing in the world" and then display my birth story as some sort of a victor's trophy. I also thought God would be more pleased with me if I did things "his way," so I was determined to earn his love and approval by avoiding an epidural. Being in a lot of pain seemed more spiritual. As you read in the first chapter,

I endured a traumatic labor and overdosed on Pitocin without any pain relief. I emerged from the experience defeated and exhausted, rather than a triumphant victor.

We strive for happiness, personal freedom, and more comfortable lives. Pain serves as an interruption at best, a devastating crisis that crumbles everything at worst, but we rarely think of pain as having purpose. We quickly seek panaceas to avoid pain or discomfort. We feel that pain is bad, wrong, and evil—across the board. We'll do what we need to do to avoid it or get rid of it, even and especially in childbirth. For those of us who like to go against the grain, we may feel a sense of triumph or elitism over "weak people" when we do endure pain. Throughout the history of Christianity, there have been several ascetic movements that sought to beat the body (which was regarded as bad) to free the spirit (which was regarded as good). But God created bodies—they are good, and will be resurrected. God is not pleased when we starve them, hurt them, or injure them; he wants us to respect and care for them.

I gave birth to my first child without an epidural, but the experience didn't provide the satisfaction I sought. I became more fearful of pain in other areas of my life, and my fear led me to adopt a position of avoidance—avoidance of pain, relationships, difficult emotions, and even hope, because hopes unfulfilled can break a heart.

I carried my avoidance through the birth of my second child 19 months later, asking for an epidural right away. Although epidurals may serve a good purpose in labor, my reason for wanting an epidural was not a good one. I was still wallowing in the disappointment and terror of my first birth, so I made the choice purely out of fear and avoidance of pain—something that marked many other choices in my life at that time. My first childbirth experience negatively impacted my soul much more than I expected—but birth is powerful enough to do that.

Before continuing any farther, we need to discuss the terms we'll use for the pain and suffering of labor, because the Bible uses the metaphor of childbirth to describe some types of suffering.

Many birth professionals do not like these words for childbirth; words influence our perceptions, and if a woman goes into labor expecting to experience the worst pain of her life, her experience will likely conform to her expectations as she fights against each contraction. Many childbirth educators change their vocabulary to reflect this mind-body connection, using words like "waves" rather than "contractions" and "pressure" rather than "pain." These words can easily become insincere euphemisms.

But suffering and childbirth commonly interact in Scripture. The interplay of themes appears often enough to teach us something quite useful and honest: For many women throughout history, childbirth has brought anxiety, pain, exhaustion, surprise, loss of control, and fear. Because of this, it serves as a fitting metaphor, since these emotions and sensations are common to other life challenges. Birthing philosophies that use different words to describe sensations are fine, so long as they don't encourage dishonesty about the actual experience.

In the biblical story, suffering resembles childbirth in that (1) it will come to an end at some point, and (2) it will result in new life that gives the suffering meaning. If you find yourself in agony and grief in labor, then plant yourself within the story of Scripture. The biblical writers are not shy or dishonest about hardship, and they tell stories of suffering as springboards to hope and new life. If you find that your labor is easier than you expected, painless, or even orgasmic, then you can certainly rejoice in God's grace to you! But these are not the images of childbirth used in the Bible;[2] followers of God frequently find themselves in places of suffering, awaiting their delivery in hope. Metaphors are not meant to encompass all experiences of all people; they simply paint a picture to convey a message.

I discuss pain and suffering almost interchangeably in this chapter, though they are not exactly the same thing; they're two sides of the same coin. Although not all suffering includes physical pain, suffering is difficult because it at least includes the emotional pain of grief, agony, and fear. In childbirth, there can be both the physical pain of labor and emotional agony brought on by fear and anxiety. Both physical and emotional pain—in childbirth and other areas of suffering in life—can often be reduced with good training for the heart and body. Not all pain, emotional or physical, is experienced as suffering in childbirth. As we will discuss, if we focus on how certain pains or even emotional distress are ultimately benefitting us, we may experience them not as suffering but as something working for our good.

While studies show that unmedicated, intervention-free childbirth is the safest option for most low-risk, healthy mothers and babies, there are situations where the benefits of pain medications in labor may outweigh the risks. Epidurals can lower high blood pressure, provide an exhausted mother with rest so she can continue the hard work of labor, and give effective relief if the pain is overwhelming. Labor is hard, and it is harder for some women than others. Pelvic shape, position of the baby, positions of the mother, size of the baby, pain threshold of the mother, how supportive the birth environment is—these are just a few of the many factors that play into the mother's perceived pain, and they may be different each time the same woman gives birth! Epidurals and other common pain relief for labor can sometimes restore dignity, energy, and hope, or prevent trauma.[3]

I am not encouraging guilt or shame for those who choose to have an epidural or other pain relief. Labor is hard work, often made much harder by modern medical protocols for labor. There is no condemnation here for women who seek out or accept offers for pain medications. I think Jesus is much less concerned with whether women have epidurals, elective C-sections, or orgasmic deliveries in the woods than he is with the hearts of the women giving birth.

Pain with Purpose

When I ask women why they chose or are planning an epidural childbirth, the overwhelming response is, "Why suffer if I don't have to?" There are three underlying assumptions here: (1) suffering is meaningless and should be avoided always, (2) escape from pain is entirely possible in childbirth, and (3) all childbirth is suffering. We'll explore each of these assumptions in turn.

Is Suffering Meaningless?

If we hold to prevailing Western cultural attitudes, we see pain as randomly affecting poor souls in the universe, with no beneficial outcome. I could recount statistics about the number of cancer diagnoses per year or how many suffer from chronic hunger or the number of victims of human trafficking—just a few of the horrors in our world. We all know the numbers of people who suffer are very high—our eyes tend to glaze over at the statistics—but in general, those people are strangers to us. The numbers begin to mean much more to us when we are one of them, or when someone we love becomes part of that number, and it often sends us reeling. We suddenly wonder where God is in all of it if we ourselves have been taken down. If God loved us, wouldn't he prevent our suffering? If suffering is meaningless, then it only makes sense that God would take away pain, out of his love for us.

While critics of Christianity may accuse Christians of being "pie in the sky" people, much of Scripture is actually focused on suffering. The Bible begins in the Garden and explains where suffering came from—sin entering the world, bringing death and destruction into God's good creation. The climax of the story is the birth, death, and resurrection of the Suffering Servant promised to Israel to bless the whole world. The Bible ends with the death of death— at the hands of a slaughtered Lamb who is also victorious Lion. In between, people who follow God with great faith (and sometimes not-so-great faith) find themselves wandering in the wilderness, sold into slavery, wrongfully imprisoned, oppressed, exiled, and persecuted (Heb 11:32–40). For the people of God, suffering is the *norm*, not the exception.

Suffering is embedded within the story of Scripture and given great meaning. Scripture tells us that God is present with us in our sufferings; that God uses suffering to transform us to be more like his Son, who suffered to bring us life; and that he will one day give an expiration date for our "How long, O Lord?" prayers. Scripture tells us that we endure hardship as discipline from God, knowing that it means we are his children, "in order that we may share in his holiness" (Heb 12:10). Suffering with God produces endurance, maturity, and wisdom (Jas 1:2–4). No suffering is meaningless, and no suffering occurs apart from the watchful and caring eyes and ears of God (Pss 17:6–9; 18:6; see also Matt 6:25–34). We have been united with Christ; his suffering is now ours, and ours is his. If we are not deeply and firmly planted within this story ourselves, then we will find ourselves in utter chaos when adversity comes.

Pain itself is not bad. Sure, it doesn't *feel good*, but that is no true indication that it is bad. Pain is a protective mechanism that God wired into our bodies. If we had no pain, we might keep our hand on a hot stove until it was burned beyond repair, keep running on a broken leg until it became useless, or allow a ruptured appendix to fester and become gangrenous. Pain is a signal that makes us stop and pay attention to our bodies so that we can take care of them. In this sense pain is actually a good thing, as is our desire to get rid of it or avoid it.

In normal childbirth, pain serves a good use. Professor of midwifery Nicky Leap interviewed a panel of 10 midwives, who had considerable experience in home birth without pharmaceutical interventions, on their views about pain in childbirth. The interviews revealed two prominent paradigms concerning pain. The first paradigm is the most common: Pain is bad, an enemy to be avoided or fought against. The second, held by the midwives and many of their clients, was that pain was something to be *worked with*, an aid to labor and delivery.[4] Pain tells a woman that labor is about to begin; this signal enables her to find a safe place to give birth. When the brain gets the signal that the body is in pain, it produces beta-endorphins,[5] natural painkillers, and other hormones that help a woman cope with labor as the intensity builds. In labor, the pain gives clues as to how the woman is doing and where she is in the process. Sharp pains in the cervix mean that it is dilating, opening wide to make room for the baby. Deep pressure in the bottom and the stretching of the perineum until it burns means that the moment of delivery is arriving. Pain can even act as a message from the baby to the mother to change her position to make birth easier. Pain in the lower back might be alleviated by the mother getting on her hands and knees, encouraging the baby to rotate into a more advantageous position that allows her to move through the pelvis rather than into the rear pelvic bones. Pain is never meaningless in birth. If the mother tunes herself into the pain rather than avoiding it, she can work with the pain to make childbirth faster and easier and risk fewer interventions, like forceps delivery, episiotomy, or C-section.

This is true for births that have unexpected complications, too. Discomfort is normal, but if the pain becomes so extreme that the mother manage it, it may mean that something isn't right and needs to be investigated. Certain pains in certain places can help caregivers find the root of the problem more quickly. Although the pain hurts, these signals are vital for early intervention when necessary. Pain after childbirth is normal and good, compelling women to rest and recover, helping the uterus return to its original size, or alerting mothers when milk might be clogging a duct in the breast before it turns into mastitis. Pain hurts, but it protects us. When we habitually numb ourselves to pain, we may inadvertently prevent finding and solving the underlying problem.

Escaping the Pain?

The second myth we may believe about childbirth and pain is that, if we receive the epidural, narcotics, or tranquilizers that are offered, we can escape the pain of childbirth entirely. Unfortunately, this isn't true. In my second birth, I had painful back labor and chose an epidural early on to avoid the pain I felt in my first birth.[6] I slept through much of active labor and woke up to push the baby out. There was some intense pressure, but nothing I'd describe as pain, thanks to the epidural. It was a much more peaceful and dignified birth experience compared to my first. Best of all, I thought I'd avoided most of the pain. What I didn't expect is that it made the afterpains of birth seem much more painful, because I hadn't worked up to managing contractions as I would have in an unmedicated birth. I also didn't have the aid of the endorphins and oxytocin that the body produces in response to normal labor. The afterpains were like a second labor, except this time no one was offering me an epidural, and everyone kept handing me a newborn to take care of and urging me to walk the halls to wake my body back up after the epidural. As it turned out, while I thought was *avoiding* pain, I was only delaying it.

Epidurals tend to drive up the need for instrumental deliveries by forceps or vacuum extraction, as the mother is lying down and cannot use gravity or her pelvic muscles to push effectively. Forceps increase the risk of birth injury to both mother and baby, causing painful tears, perineal damage, or urinary incontinence for months after the birth, as well as bruises or swelling for the baby. For about one in five women, epidurals cause long-term backache well after the birth. Epidurals also may increase the need for cesarean sections, which are major abdominal surgeries. There may be tremendous pain at the incision site for weeks, as well as painful trapped intestinal gas. This is all pain experienced *after* the birth. For many women, avoiding pain may be only delaying pain.

I recommend learning and practicing coping mechanisms for pain in labor, even if you fully intend to have an epidural. You will not be permitted to have an epidural until you reach a certain point in your labor, and you never know if you will have to go without an epidural. Your labor may progress too quickly, the anesthesiologist may not be immediately available, and in some cases, the epidural may not work for your body.[7] It's smart to know how to manage pain in and after labor, since "escaping" it—even if for a short while—may not always be realistic. Gritting your teeth and bearing it is not a good plan for anyone and only increases your perception of pain. A good childbirth education class can provide you with these tools. An online search can help you find classes in your area, or your caregiver might recommend good classes near you.

For much of life, there is no way out but through. Childbirth can teach us to face pain head-on, to submit ourselves to our loving God in the tempest, and to find life and resurrection on the other side. God can use labor to train us in sticking through something hard. It's a vital lesson to learn. How many people do you know who spend their years stewing in resentment? How many do you know who self-medicate with alcohol or porn or other addictions, avoiding their own pain? I don't want to become someone who cannot face hard things well. We cannot avoid or truly escape suffering—it comes to us in all kinds of forms throughout life. As we turn to face our suffering, trusting in God to care for us no matter what comes and grounding ourselves in Christ, we also submit ourselves for training in endurance through trials.

Childbirth as Training for Endurance

The third myth is that all childbirth is suffering—a trial to endure and merely survive. When birth is approached as a curse to bear, it becomes one. In other areas of our lives, we willingly, if not joyfully, submit ourselves to discomfort, pain, pressure, and risk of injury to achieve a goal. I have a friend who is an ultramarathon runner with several 50- and 100-mile races under her very tiny belt. She loves the exhilaration of a new challenge, of making goals and training for success, and of finally achieving them. She has sacrificed her toenails, many pairs of running shoes, and hours upon hours every week for these goals. On a less extreme scale, mere mortals like me who run 5ks train for them, knowing they may endure blisters, sore muscles, or injury. They build up their endurance and strength over time and find they are able to endure longer runs.

In many ways, becoming pregnant can be like signing up for a marathon or a 5k. There is some training time before the big day, and if we don't train for it, we might be sucking air and panicking right from the start. We might dread that day if we know we aren't ready. But if we willingly submit ourselves to train for the race, to build up our endurance and prepare our minds and bodies and hearts for the long haul, then the outcome will be so much better. If I didn't train for a 5k, I might run that race and finish it, but I would have an experience of suffering for sure. If I do train for it, it may still be difficult. But I'm more likely to see it as a feat of endurance rather than a trial to fight through.

We can view birthing pains as a training ground in endurance, strength building, and working with pain rather than avoiding it. It can be an exercise against escapism and denial, instead teaching us to see purpose in pain when we've been taught to think of pain as meaningless. Our brains are brilliant at interpreting sensations and giving them meaning. If you believe childbirth is a curse to suffer through, then you will interpret each contraction, every stretching sensation, and every bit of pressure as dangerous pain threatening to destroy you. You just have to birth that baby before it kills you! However, there are better interpretations of pain and sensations. You can interpret the sensations as normal, and you can identify *that* sensation as a contraction that is aiding your baby to move into the world, and *that* twinge as your cervix opening wider to allow safe passage, and *that* overwhelming pressure as a sign that you are almost there. Then the pain is no longer a threat, and you can relax and let it do its work. If you equate childbirth with a race you have prepared for, expecting certain pains and sensations and mental blocks that are normal for most racers, then it is no longer interpreted as suffering.

Childbirth is different from other types of suffering in that, while it may be painful and emotionally agonizing for many women, it has an end point—one that is relatively soon after it begins. Labor is short term, and even within labor, there are natural reprieves. Contractions usually last only 30 to 90 seconds, followed by breaks of between 1 and 20 minutes, depending on how close the mother is to delivering her baby. These breaks are generally painless, and the mother can rest, move around, relax, and get her bearings. Even in the most intense part of labor, there are breaks.[8] Some of the worst suffering in the world is horrible precisely because there are no reprieves, no end in sight, and no apparent purpose. Childbirth is actually a cause for rejoicing—a baby is coming into the world! Childbirth, then, is generally not deep suffering in the traditional sense of the concept.

The Bible uses the imagery of childbirth to describe some aspects of suffering, both physical and emotional, as we saw in chapter 4. When men suddenly received bad news of impending doom, they are described as being seized with pain, agony, or even terror, as a woman is seized with birth pains. People are described as writhing and groaning in agony as women in labor. Trembling, limp hands and loss of strength, and fear for the events to come are common themes (Psa 48:5–6; Isa 13:8; 21:3; Jer 6:24; 13:21; 30:6; 49:21–24; 50:43; Mic 4:9–10). These feelings and experiences are common to childbirth—especially during a time when education and advanced medical care were not as readily available—and are useful for conveying the emotions of sudden suffering.

When childbirth doesn't proceed normally, and when the suffering has gone from normal birth pangs to massive abdominal surgery, stillbirth, an unexpected disability, or any traumatic experience—if we have trained our minds, hearts, and bodies to be ready to hold anchor, they will. The waves may crash hard over us, threaten to dislodge us, and keep coming with hurricane force for a long time. If we hold on to Jesus in it all, knowing he is good and that he suffers with us and there is purpose in it all, then we can survive the pain. And that's the hardest thing about life—hanging on in hope through intense pain. It's why we need all the training we can get. Childbirth doesn't weatherproof us for everything we may face, but it can strengthen our inner resilience muscles and provide a metaphor for us in other seasons of life.

The Western "damsel in distress" motif of a weak woman in need of rescue from her pain by knights in white has no place in the delivery room. It encourages passivity, fear, and loss of control. Proverbs 31 speaks of a noble wife worth more than rubies. She is not the 1950s housewife that we often superimpose upon the passage, but a strong woman full of valor, industry, strength, and wisdom. The passage says nothing of childbirth, but we can imagine what it would look like for a woman of courage and strength to give birth. She does not escape or avoid hard things, but she faces them and trusts her God to transform her through them.

As followers of Jesus, we know that women of strength are not those who endure pain without epidurals or who survive hard things. Strong women are those who are rooted in the strength of Jesus. Strong women receive *his* strength in their weakness—in the moment of transition, in the emergency operation, in the postpartum journey, in the loss and devastation and joy. Childbirth is so variable, unpredictable. We need encouragement to seek first not the perfect birth, healing birth, or painless birth—we need encouragement to seek first Jesus, who carries us through in his strength no matter how our birth story pans out.

Normal childbirth teaches us to live awake to all parts of life, rather than turning to our natural desire for numbness. Childbirth is, in many ways, much easier than many things we will face in life. For a relatively small percentage, childbirth does pose a risk of injury or death. This is the reality of the brokenness of our world. But for most healthy, childbearing women, normal childbirth is possible and can be achieved without surgery or anything worse. There are parts of our lives that are *not* this safe! Childbirth puts us face-to-face with our mortality, and every pregnant woman has to wrestle with fear. We have to face these dangers head-on, or they may destroy us when they catch us off guard. What do you fear? If you do confront your fears, will they have any power over you?

As each contraction becomes stronger and more powerful, it can become part of our spiritual formation in Christ. We yield ourselves and our fears to God so that he can train us in endurance through pain rather than avoiding pain. Our avoidance of painful or difficult-to-understand emotions and memories has led us to become a people of addictions: to social media, TV, food, porn, work and productivity, the Internet, alcohol, shopping, others' approval. Our addictions comfort us in the short term, gratify us in the moments when we begin to feel emotional pain, and help us hold it off a while longer. It feels much easier to binge on Netflix movies than slog through our loneliness, anger, sadness, or emptiness. If we seek to routinely numb ourselves from pain in life, then we are living in fear. Childbirth provides a training ground to combat our natural tendencies to flee discomfort, and it provides the motivation to do this out of love for someone other than ourselves. Could it be that God has designed childbirth to be something that trains women for endurance in hardship in a life that presents many hardships? Could it be that God has created childbirth to make women more like Jesus?

Followers of Jesus are not to be marked by fear, not even in childbirth:

> We know and rely on the love God has for us.
> God is love. Whoever lives in love lives in God, and God in them. This is how love is made complete among us so that we will have confidence on the day of judgment: In this world we are like Jesus. There is no fear in love. But perfect love drives out fear, because fear has to do with punishment. The one who fears is not made perfect in love.
> We love because he first loved us (1 John 4:16–19).

In this world, we endure things that Jesus endured: we pick up our cross, we experience suffering for the sake of others, and we lay down our lives out of love. This is the life of a person who follows Jesus, and we can do this hard thing because "perfect love drives out fear."

Jesus was afraid. In his distress, "his sweat was like drops of blood" on the night before his death (Luke 22:44). He called his closest friends to stay awake and pray with him, and he experienced loneliness and cried out in despair for God to take this cup from him. But his perfect love drove out fear, and he didn't make his choice to submit to the cross out of fear. He made it out of love. And this love is made complete in us when we live as Jesus did, submitting our lives to love and not fear.

A mother endures much for the love of her children—in childbirth she endures pain to bring the child into the world, and in parenting she sacrifices comfort, time, sleep, ambition, and more. Perfect love, while sacrificial, does not parade around in a spirit of martyrdom. Many mothers have to fight against self-pity. Sometimes the busyness of our lives with young children or the magnitude of constant sacrifices makes us feel more important. Childbirth can become a competition of comparative sacrifice:

how long labor lasted or how painful it was—the worse it is, the more a mother can cling to her crown of martyrdom.

The temptation is there in parenthood, too, as mothers consider the loss of quiet or perhaps an income as they envy the "easy" lives of child-free friends. Perfect love in the way of Jesus puts the interests of others above our own, so that we are not pitiful martyrs but those who press on in the strength of Jesus, giving our lives in service to the "least of these" (Matt 25:40). Clark and Johnson write, "The redeemed image Christ's glory as we share in his descent of self-giving love, as we freely spend ourselves that others might flourish, and as we joyfully discover, perhaps to our repeated surprise, that self-emptying and self-fulfillment are not antithetical, but identical (Matt. 16:24–25; Mark 8:34–35)."[9]

In her book *Great with Child*, Debra Rienstra meditates on the ways that the Christian's redemptive view of blood connects us with the suffering of Christ in childbirth and even menstruation. She writes:

> We women don't shed blood for sins, ours or other people's. But we do shed it, typically, amid some sadness, and we do shed it for the possibility of new life. Does this not give us a kind of connection to Jesus that has been very little discussed or appreciated, a kind of automatic stigmata? Because I see Christ's bleeding at the center of redemptive history, can I also see women's bleeding resonate outward from this, across all ages and history and races of women? Peasant farmers and student protesters, wealthy landowners and corporate managers, refugees and homesteaders, tribal matriarchs and factory workers—wherever women participated in the world and suffered its blows, our bleeding testifies to pain and hope, uncannily combined.[10]

Because we are united with Christ, even in our menstrual cycles and birth stories—the gore and the mess and the life of it—can point us to his suffering, his love, and his life. Perhaps women's bleeding could keep us from the sentimental religion that

Christianity is often reduced to—little more than self-help or so-cial activism, with Jesus as the mascot. The blood reminds us that holiness is not something we earn but something given to us, shed amid great sorrow and sadness but bringing life where previously there was only death.

Waiting in Hope of the Resurrection

Laboring in endurance teaches us our limits—physical as well as emotional. Very commonly, a woman will reach a point in her la-bor where she may cry out or think, "I cannot do this!" This mo-ment of extreme despair is often reached soon before the baby is born—a stage called transition. Just after despair, the mother sud-denly finds renewed energy and strength, aided by the adrenaline rush that occurs at this moment, just in time to push her baby out into the world.

These moments of desperation and despair come to us in life in other ways. In 2014, a dear friend of mine was diagnosed with post-traumatic stress disorder. She went through intense counsel-ing to peel back the layers of many past abuses and traumas that she had avoided for years. She had horrific, violent nightmares and flashbacks that paralyzed her. She had panic attacks almost constantly, and her deep depression left her barely functional. As she and her counselor continued for several months and she was able to open deeper wounds, it only got worse. She was in ut-ter despair, certain that she would never function normally again. One day she cried out in hopelessness to me, "I just can't do it anymore!" And then, soon after, the panic attacks came less fre-quently. The nightmares dropped off, and the flashbacks no lon-ger controlled her. It wasn't that she had figured out how to not think about the hard things anymore; it was that she had gotten through to the other side. At the moment she believed she couldn't push through another second, she suddenly did and found new life. There was no way out but through.

Childbirth is used in Scripture as a metaphor for the suffering of God's people as they await delivery in hope. Various biblical writ-ers often speak of trials and persecutions in terms of labor, like contractions that squeeze and push and cause anxiety. But the point of these passages is that the Day of the Lord is coming, that these sufferings result in new life being born from the old. In John 16, Jesus tells his disciples that he is about to die and they will grieve, but then he will be raised again to life. He says, "You will weep and mourn while the world rejoices. You will grieve, but your grief will turn to joy. A woman giving birth to a child has pain because her time has come; but when her baby is born she forgets the anguish because of her joy that a child is born into the world" (16:20–21). Jesus speaks of grief and pain as temporary sorrows that will at some point give way to new life and joy. Here he uses the clear metaphor of childbirth to put his death and the disciples' grief in proper perspective: These birth pangs must happen so that new life can be birthed.

Paul likewise talks about creation being in the pains of childbirth, as well as our own groans as we await our adoption (Rom 8:18–27). These pains and groans will someday birth new creation, "liberated from its bondage to decay and brought into the freedom and glory of the children of God" (8:21). He goes on to describe the redemption of our bodies as being birthed from the pains of the present time and says that we should wait patiently in this hope.

We need these moments of getting through to the other side as memorials in our lives, pillars to look at and remember our darkest trials of life. Childbirth provides such a milestone, where we can look back and say, "Yes, I've been here in despair before, right where I wanted to quit, and I endured and saw life on the other side." Those moments provide us with a precedent for the future.

This relationship we build with Jesus through labor will enable us to wait with him in hope for new life on the other side. If we follow Jesus, we know that we have willingly taken up a cross and persecution and trials. But with the cross, we also lay hold of resurrection.

The Bible uses the metaphor of birth for suffering that brings new life—because this is what the Bible is about. Birth pangs are not merely pain; they are forces that push new life out of the old. When passages of Scripture speak of God crying out in the pains of childbirth, they highlight God's creative power and "signal a new phase of creative intervention in the lives of her people."[11] Isaiah records God's words:

> For a long time I have kept silent,
>   I have been quiet and held myself back.
> But now, like a woman in childbirth,
>   I cry out, I gasp and pant.
> I will lay waste the mountains and hills
>   and dry up all their vegetation;
> I will turn rivers into islands
>   and dry up the pools.
> I will lead the blind by ways they have not known,
>   along unfamiliar paths I will guide them;
> I will turn the darkness into light before them
>   and make the rough places smooth (42:14–16).

It may be difficult for us to think of the travails of childbirth as a symbol of power, creativity, and new birth when we are used to confining it to the pointless pain of a curse. But even God writhes in labor in his creative power to bring life.

Paul writes to the Galatians as a mother in labor: "My dear children, for whom I am again in the pains of childbirth until Christ is formed in you, how I wish I could be with you now and change my tone, because I am perplexed about you!" (Gal 4:19–20). Paul is frustrated that the Galatians are being taken in by Judaizers, and he is setting their theology straight in this letter. He describes his situation as a mother in childbirth—simultaneously affectionate with mother love for the baby, frustrated and perhaps even angry with the baby for the slow labor, longing for the new birth, writhing and working in pain for delivery. Paul describes their discipleship in terms of labor and says that the birth will happen when "Christ is formed in you." The pain has purpose, and Paul presses into it with the love of a mother for her child.

The body has its own versions of death and resurrection in labor. The despair and anguish of transition, the stage just before pushing, is like a small death: Adrenaline is high, and you simply cannot imagine going on. You may even feel that you're experiencing your death. The fear, agony, adrenaline, anxiety, and contractions then give way—and a baby is born! Ask almost any mother, and she will tell you that whatever pain she felt in childbirth, she would do so again many times for the love of that child. I've supported many women in labor who, at transition, were begging for a cesarean, and just minutes after giving birth, were talking about giving birth to the *next* baby! The hormonal high of oxytocin just following childbirth is the highest in a woman's lifetime, giving her incredible renewed energy even after the most exhausting labor, overwhelming her with feelings of love and euphoria.[12] It seems that God has hardwired our childbearing bodies with hope of new life following suffering—after all, this is what the story of the world is all about.

The gospel is imprinted in the drama of childbirth—in the anxiety and agony of childbearing, which increased because of sin; in the birth of the Child who would live, die, and rise again to rescue us and crush the serpent's head. We feel in our bodies the suffering that sin has caused, we pass through it, and we feel the joy and triumph of resurrection and new life in our arms. We experience the birth pangs that all of creation groans with in anticipation of Christ's return, grunting and pushing for heaven to break through. Childbirth, in its mess and toil and joy, points us to Jesus in his risen glory. "Praise be to the God and Father of our Lord Jesus Christ! In his great mercy he has given us *new birth* into a living hope through the resurrection of Jesus Christ from the dead, and into an inheritance that can never perish, spoil or fade" (1 Pet 1:3–4).

Husbands and Birth Supporters

Those who support the mother in labor have an opportunity for soul training, too. How many times do we sit beside a loved one in pain, feeling helpless and useless? We may feel that because we cannot provide relief, comfort, or the right words, that it really is not useful for us to be present and engaged with the person. Sitting with a laboring mother may provide this same feeling for those who are not medical attendants. We wonder whether we are in the way since we provide no seemingly useful services or skills.

The answer, of course, is, no. Women in labor and loved ones who suffer may not be able to articulate it—or they may even use you as a target to offset their pain—but they draw strength from your presence. We need each other in these hard moments, even though the moments may be uncomfortably silent. The labor room has typically been reserved for women only—husbands remaining with their wives in childbirth is a radically new idea even in American culture and still is not practiced in much of the world. How comforting to be surrounded by women who not only have loved you for years but also have been exactly where you are now? Their words in your despair carry weight—they got to the other side of where you are now.

In the same way, Jesus, our high priest, endured the suffering and pain of the cross to reach the other side. He endured the life we live, and he is full of grace because of it. He intercedes for us now, as one who knows our weakness and understands (Heb 4:14–15). No, he didn't go through physiological childbirth as a mother. But as we have seen, there are passages that describe God as in the throes of labor with his people. If God knows anguish, surely he knows anguish more than we do. If Jesus is the Suffering Servant who endures pain for the love of his people, then a mother could relate to that sacrificial love on a smaller scale, couldn't she?

So in our anguished moments—whether in childbirth or in other parts of our lives—we can approach the throne of grace with confidence, knowing we will receive grace to help in our time of need (Heb 4:16). Childbirth can be a training ground where we remind ourselves of Jesus' union with us in his humanity and his ministry now of listening to our prayers and granting us grace when we need it—especially in our weakness.

For husbands and other birth supporters who have not personally given birth, coming alongside a woman in labor carries tremendous value. Simple gestures—like offering a sip of water, providing a needed back massage, or a loving word when despair sets in—can carry a woman through her weakest moments. Laboring mothers need to be reminded of God's love and goodness, of the hope and resurrection on the other side of the despair. In this way, even those who are with a woman in her labor can be transformed as they learn to wait with others in their trials, as they have an opportunity to forego food, sleep, and comfort to support someone who is vulnerable—actions that are done as for Jesus himself (Matt 25:37-40). These simple gestures of encouragement and support can make all the difference to a laboring woman as she reaches for hope and strength.

Most of us may not be able to fully escape pain in labor. None of us will escape pain in life. Submitting ourselves to the care of our creator in childbirth can act as practice for when hardships come and endurance through suffering is needed, knowing that birth pangs give way to transformation and new life. Instead of seeking escape, may we root ourselves deeply in him, holding fast to him whatever may come, in labor and in life.

Spiritual Disciplines for Chapter 5

In chapter 5, we countered the ideas that God's favor can somehow be earned by enduring pain and that we can fully avoid or escape pain in labor or in life. God uses pain in childbirth to train us in endurance, in suffering with hope, knowing that his story enfolds us and, thus, our pain is given purpose and meaning. All suffering has an end point, and for Christians, it ends with the emergence of new life and resurrection.

Now we turn to the spiritual disciplines of lament and fasting, two often-avoided practices in our culture, which exalts comfort and doing "what feels right." While these practices will look different during pregnancy, labor, and postpartum, finding ways to engage them will exercise those resilience muscles and train us for endurance in the future.

Lament

In this chapter, we explored biblical imagery of childbirth that also depicts suffering. The suddenness of grief, and the overwhelming and unstoppable despair that accompanies it, can leave a person groaning, panting, and trembling like a woman in labor. The metaphor of childbirth is especially useful for God's people, because while we may mourn and groan in this world, new life awaits us on the other side. The pain has a purpose and is never meaningless, both as we give birth and as we walk through the trials of this life. God uses pain for our transformation, to grow us in wisdom and holiness, and sometimes for the good of others.

If you live long enough, you will experience pain and sorrow. The rich tradition of lament in the Scriptures acknowledges this reality and cries out to God over it, though we ourselves may avoid pain or deny its existence. In the discipline of lament we bring our sufferings, pain, and complaints to God in worship. Many of us tend to think complaining or dwelling on hardships is the opposite of worship. We are quick to paint silver linings around our clouds, though we may be living dishonestly before God in an attempt to avoid hard things.

Never is this more apparent than at funerals. My mother and brother both died far too young and in terrible ways. Yet at their funerals, it seemed that everyone glazed over the deep loss and hurt and offered "the bright side." Their funerals were more like celebrations than laments, and it felt dishonest and lonely. Lament leans us right into the pain, making us feel the force of what is inside us, so that we cannot escape or avoid it any longer. Lament allows us to open ourselves before God as we cry out to him with our questions, complaints, and anger. Grief is hard work, but it is the only way to get through to the other side of the despair. We cannot skip the labor!

When we labor through lament, we don't know when it will end, when birth will finally happen. Lamenting with God over time creates trust, and it deepens further if we can lament with other believers before God. Worship in the church should be a mingling of both praise and lament; we serve a great and loving God, but we will often walk in rough places until Jesus returns. Pretending the pain doesn't exist doesn't make a holier person; it creates an angry and lonely person who wears a mask before God and others. Lament brings us into new humility because we have to acknowledge that we are not strong enough on our own, that we don't have all the answers—and that makes us vulnerable.

Prayer is an integral part of lament. Our prayers weave in and out of our groaning, and they keep us from distancing ourselves from God in our hurts. How much, each day, do you entrust yourself to God through prayer? Do you take minor anxieties, upsets, and changes of plan and bring them to God? Or do you find yourself in fits of anger and frustration because things aren't going your way? Do you feel that he listens to your prayers even when you don't need a miracle? Do you pray when you aren't desperate? If prayer is not a reflex when things are good, it will not be a reflex in suffering. He is trustworthy in our good lives and in our broken lives.

In childbirth, we have a practical outlet for lament in our perceived suffering (remember, not all childbirth is suffering!). Childbirth teaches us to anchor ourselves to Jesus for strength and endurance through hardship. As we labor we join in the long story of those who have groaned before God, awaiting deliverance. We groan and ground ourselves in our bodies, not escaping them or pretending the pain doesn't exist. If we cry out to God rather than fighting pain as an enemy, we release ourselves to God's care and find new life on the other side. Lament allows us to move through the process of grief in pain and suffering rather than remaining in it, letting us reach the other side. Biblical lament gives us to space to move around in our hurt, to explore it and feel it and sit in it until we are able to move on. The psalmists often interlace their mourning with unexpected praise and spontaneous moments of hope. As they bring their suffering before God, they find renewal little by little and are reminded of hope in the midst of their grief for those who belong to God.

Fasting

The discipline of fasting is no longer a popular one. Although it is commanded by God throughout Scripture to people who lived in much less abundance than most of us do, we seem to have an idea that a day without food will leave us malnourished and unhealthy. Fasting is a spiritual exercise where we abstain from something, usually food and drinks other than water, to focus our energy on God. In Scripture, people often fasted in times of desperate repentance or grief. Often, fasting accompanies prayer and seems to increase the power of those prayers, accelerating God's purposes in certain situations. Jesus fasted in the wilderness just prior to the beginning of his ministry, and he often retreated in prayer to lonely places. Fasting teaches us not to be slaves to whatever we are fasting from, and it is a sometimes-difficult exercise in endurance to accomplish a spiritual goal.

Fasting is a way of subjecting ourselves to discomfort so that we are not slaves to our own comfort. (As Paul notes in 1 Corinthians 9:27, disciplining our bodies relates to spiritual discipline, as it teaches us self-control.) Fasting is a tangible exercise in working *with* hardship rather than fighting against it, for transformation by God. Fasting, in a variety of forms, can teach us humility, dependence on God, trust, and working hard to seek him—skills that benefit women in labor as well as anyone who lives through pain. While pregnant or nursing, it is generally not recommended to fast from food. But pregnancy brings up the opportunity to fast from many things—some activities, certain harmful foods, medications, cigarettes, or alcohol. Many of these things are not truly difficult to give up if we know they may harm our babies, though every woman is different. Pregnancy itself can often be a test of endurance, especially in the final weeks, where a woman may be so miserable that she would do anything to get that baby out! Engaging in a fast allows us to intentionally grow in endurance through hardship with God.

Exercises for Lament and Fasting

1. Is there pain or grief you've been avoiding? The practice of lament can teach us to bring our pain before God and can help us to wait in hope. Praying the Scriptures can give us the vocabulary we may need for complaining and crying out to God. Psalms 13, 22, 39, and 56 are good places to start (though there are many laments throughout Scripture!). Read a lamenting passage slowly, several times. Allow yourself to feel what you have been avoiding, and bring this brokenness to God without cushioning any of it. You may find you need the words of these laments in labor as you await delivery in hope.

2. Pregnancy and childbirth, because of the fall, are laced with danger. Women have to face their fears in childbirth. For many women, especially in the West, childbirth is not truly dangerous. But we live in a world tinged by death and danger. Tell God your fears. Make a resolution to entrust your life to your Creator, no matter what may come. If the worst happens, do you believe it will be because God has abandoned you or because you did something wrong and he is punishing you?

Rather than avoiding your deepest fears, confront them. Find passages of Scripture that remind you of who God is and who you are in him. Tell yourself the truth now, so that you don't have to scramble to find it later. Train your mind to trust and love God, because the enemy inundates us with lies when hardship comes. Ask God to show you how you are being motivated by fear instead of love.

3. Prepare yourself for managing pain in labor. Whether you plan for an epidural or a drug-free birth, you do not know exactly how things will go, so you need to be prepared to manage some level of pain. Attend a good birth-skills class and learn the mechanics of deep breathing, relaxation, and releasing yourself to God and his work of getting your baby out through contractions. This may not seem like a spiritual practice, but learning to manage anxiety, pain, and fear as they manifest themselves physically has a tremendous impact on your emotional ability to handle hardship.

4. In many countries, childbirth is fraught with much suffering due to poverty, malnutrition, poor education, disease, lack of contraception, and unjust birth practices. Lament with women who face such danger with each child they birth. Cry out on their behalf to God. If you have a friend or fellow church member who recently had a miscarriage or other tragedy, sit with them if appropriate and offer laments to God in their presence.

5. Choose something to fast from for a specific amount of time. If you are pregnant or nursing, do not fast from all food without speaking to your doctor or midwife. Some other ideas include social media, chocolate, coffee, soda, eating out, shopping—choose something you do often that you would miss. Use your extra time and energy to invest in the work of prayer. Let your hunger for these things be a signal for you to hunger after God instead. Record your struggles, thoughts, feels, victories, and failures throughout your fast. Reflect on what you learned about yourself and God.

6. If you are not pregnant or nursing, and are otherwise healthy, plan a fast from food and drinks other than water. Be sure not to gorge yourself on fatty, unhealthy foods before the fast, and do not break the fast with these foods either so you don't get sick. As you hunger and long for food, consider the ways you hunger (or don't) after God. During times that would have been mealtimes, focus yourself in prayer and reading Scripture. Many people schedule a fast once a week with different goals, such as focused time with God, praying for direction and guidance, enduring in solidarity with those who suffer, or devoting time for intense prayer over something.

CHAPTER 6

God's Providence over Pregnancy and Childbirth

Yet you brought me out of the womb;
*   you made me trust in you, even at my mother's breast.*
From birth I was cast on you;
*   from my mother's womb you have been my God.*

—Psalm 22:9–10

God's Work in the Womb

If the television is on in our house, my three children sink into an alternate universe where nothing in the real world exists. In one way, it's fabulous. If I desperately need to get something done without breaking up a fight or snatching scissors from my son's hands before he snips his eyelashes, I pop in a movie and the kids fall into a wormhole until the movie is over.

One day the kids were watching a movie, and my husband came home from work, loudly shutting the door on accident. In another room, I yelled out, "Hi!" and he returned a greeting over the heads of our little darlings, who remained motionless. He walked between them and the TV to get to the next room to help me with what I was working on. Twenty minutes later the movie was over, and the kids wandered into the next room. They exclaimed, "Dad! When did you get home?" Despite their dad's volume and even walking right in front of them, my kids failed to notice what was obvious to those who were paying attention.

We often distract ourselves from God, not paying attention to the work he does on an intimate level in this world. Our blindness is self-induced. As we begin to look at pregnancy and childbirth from a biblical perspective, it is necessary for us to understand who God is and the essential role he plays in this whole process.

What Is God's Providence?

In Christianity, the doctrine of God's providence teaches that God is involved in the lives of his creatures and that those who pay attention can see evidence of this loving care in creation (Rom 1:19–20). The Heidelberg Catechism reads, "God's providence is his almighty and ever present power, whereby, as with his hand, he still upholds heaven and earth and all creatures, and so governs them that leaf and blade, rain and drought, fruitful and barren years, food and drink, health and sickness, riches and poverty, indeed, all things, come to us not by chance but by his fatherly hand."[1] God did not wind up creation like a clock and leave it to spin into chaos, abandoning humans to their own devices while he remains coldly uninvolved. Christianity understands God to be actively and continually caring for every aspect of his creation.

At one end of the spectrum of views on God's providence is the belief that God directs all processes, decisions, and minutiae toward the completion of his will. At the other end is the belief that God allows free will and knows all possibilities, but he allows wiggle room in the details. Along the spectrum between these two lie various views on how much God controls his creation, exercises his sovereignty, responds to prayer, changes his mind, and directs this world.

No matter where your view on God's sovereignty falls along this spectrum, we can all affirm that God is omnipotent, God is involved with us, and God listens to us. Colossians 1:16–17 tells us, "For in [Christ] all things were created. ... He is before all things, and in him all things hold together." Not only does he hold the universe together, but he is also attentive to you and to me. We can say with the psalmist:

> I call on you, my God, for you will answer me;
>   turn your ear to me and hear my prayer.
> Show me the wonders of your great love,
>   you who save by your right hand
>   those who take refuge in you from their foes (Psa 17:6–7).

God oversees, guides, protects, cares, and moves all of history toward that final day when he will reign over all at last.

Throughout Scripture, the biblical writers describe conception, pregnancy, and childbirth as a process that God, creator of the heavens and the earth, is intimately involved in. We will explore God's providence in conception and pregnancy first, and then in childbirth.

God's Providence in Conception and Pregnancy

David praises God for his work in David's own conception in his mother's womb:

> You created my inmost being;
>   you knit me together in my mother's womb.
> I praise you because I am fearfully and wonderfully made;
>   your works are wonderful,
>   I know that full well.
> My frame was not hidden from you
>   when I was made in the secret place,
>   when I was woven together in the depths of the earth.
> Your eyes saw my unformed body;
>   all the days ordained for me were written in your book
>   before one of them came to be (Psa 139:13–16).

Even in the dark of the womb, God was there, weaving together each part of the tiny human body. The psalmist's awe over God's wonderful work in the womb leads him to burst out in worship. Is there anyone too hidden from God, too small or insignificant for God's loving notice and care? Even the tiny embryo in his mother's womb seen by no other eye is seen by God, loved by God, and created by God.

God tells Jeremiah, "Before I formed you in the womb, I knew you, before you were born I set you apart; I appointed you as a prophet to the nations" (Jer 1:5). Isaiah spoke of God's care in forming people within their mothers' wombs (44:2, 24), as did Job (31:15). Biblical scholar Phyllis Trible notes the interesting relationship between the Hebrew words *rahamim* (compassion) and *rehem* (womb) throughout the Old Testament. In many passages, the care and control God has over the womb's activity is a sign of his mercy, loving-kindness, and divine care toward his people.[2]

God's knitting and forming and making of babies suggests an intimate knowledge of us that is surprising and unexpected. We know from biology that a fertilized zygote undergoes mitosis to divide and replicate under the direction of DNA, implants in the uterus, and receives nourishment from the placenta throughout the pregnancy as the fetus continues to form. This is all true. But when we separate biology from the God who created it and sustains it, we begin to devalue the miraculous tiny people God is forming with intimate care. We may begin to see pregnancy as chance or luck in a vast, uncaring universe, and childbirth as only the inevitable end of that process.

God's Providence in Childbirth

But separating the biological process of childbirth from recognition of God's work may tempt us to see it as a mechanistic process that can happen with or without him. Our language surrounding childbirth is an indicator of this culture of mechanistic birth. Sheila Kitzinger, an anthropologist and childbirth activist, writes that the language surrounding birth is driven by technology, mechanics, and even architectural language. Terms such as "incompetent cervix," "pubic arch," "failure to progress," and "inadequate pelvis" can communicate unintended messages about childbirth and women's bodies.[3]

The manner in which progress through labor is commonly measured—centimeters of cervical dilation per hour—often determines whether a mother is considered to be progressing well or whether her body needs pharmaceutical augmentation. This would be appropriate if women were robots who all labored according to one standard timeline, but childbirth is an organic, unique process for each woman, her body, and her baby. In this way, we may forget that each mother and baby is a beloved creature cared for and valued by God. When birth becomes standardized, women are reduced to their uteruses and the baby is reduced to a product produced by the process.

If we reduce childbirth to a robotic process, where stats are monitored and numbers are checked and charts conform to a standard, we may begin to believe we control this process. Perhaps that's why birth in Western society has become so driven by technology: We feel we are doing everything we can to control an unpredictable force. This matters for our souls because if we feel that we control birth and its outcomes, then do we need God? Or do we feel that we have this thing under control as long as we add some more savior-wires of technology?

Many birth advocates work for more control by women over their own bodies and babies in birth. I'm among them, precisely because I don't believe birth should be standardized, and I do believe women should have responsibility for their bodies and the babies they will parent. However, this straining for control needs to be balanced with a realization that our bodies and our babies belong to God. Some things in birth cannot be predicted or controlled. While educating ourselves, asking good questions of our caregivers, and giving our informed consent, we need to also entrust ourselves to our good Creator, who is sovereign over all.

The psalmist praises God for bringing him out of the womb, like a midwife:

> You brought me out of the womb;
> you made me trust in you, even at my mother's breast.
> From birth I was cast on you;
> from my mother's womb you have been my God
> (Psa 22:9–10). ·

> From birth I have relied on you;
> you brought me forth from my mother's womb.
> I will ever praise you (Psa 71:6).

God himself is described as the midwife, delivering the child from the womb and thus being trustworthy and a source of comfort. God is involved in every birth.

Since the first sin in the garden, humans have been tempted to assert our independence from God. We need to examine within ourselves our determination to birth a child through our own strength apart from God or any other kind of help, on one hand, or our dependence on technology to save us from childbirth on the other. Technology in childbirth is value-neutral—on its own, technology is neither good nor bad. Technology can save lives or endanger them, depending on a whole host of circumstances. The only dependable constant is God. We need to find ways to fix our hopes on God in all of life, even in childbirth, using technology with the wisdom God gives and drawing upon God's strength in our weakness. Only God can control unpredictable childbirth, and only he is trustworthy no matter what.

Providence and Birth Control

We are not at the mercy of mere biology, the whim of doctors, or the functional abilities of technology in childbirth. We are at the mercy of God, who is abundantly merciful. Scripture paints a picture of human fetal development that inspires—demands— worship. God is involved in this very human process, infusing sacredness into the ordinary. He made humanity and blessed them, commanding them to multiply and "fill the earth" (Gen 1:28).

Taking the blessing of fruitfulness to the extreme, some Christians believe it is wrong to deny God the avenue of blessing people with children by the use of birth control. They reject all forms of barrier and hormonal contraceptives as extensions of abortion culture, vowing to have as many children as God decides for them to have and condemning all plans to thwart pregnancy as dodging God's will. Even natural family planning, a method of charting a woman's monthly cycle and practicing abstinence during her fertile period, is equated with failing to trust God. God's work in birth is intimate and involved, but he also set the world into systems that work. If a couple has sex during a woman's fertile period, it will likely result in pregnancy. That's basic biology.

In the patriarchal, polygamous, and tribal society in which this Old Testament blessing to multiply was given, limiting family size would not have been considered wise. Life was harsh, and people struggled to survive through disease, famine, desert wanderings, and tribal conflicts. The more people to contribute to survival, the better. Further, in an honor and shame culture, more sons bring more honor and power. Barrenness was seen as shameful, which is a frequent theme in the prayers of lament and praise for women whose wombs God opened in the Bible.

This patriarchal, polygamous, tribal society is not a thing of the past; it is very much alive in the Middle East. My Arab neighbor, a bedouin woman who moved from the mountains to the city, has 10 sons and no daughters, and she is pregnant with her 11th son—a blessed Muslim woman indeed! Here in the Middle East, her status is greeted with a hearty, "Maashallah!"—literally, "God has willed it"—pronounced as a blessing (and to ward off the evil eye projected by those who might be jealous). Her family is not unusual; most women here average seven children each. But unlike most Western cultures, they also often have live-in housemaids, extended family living with them, free or low-cost health care, and a tribal culture built around this lifestyle. It is unrealistic for most Westerners to achieve this lifestyle without going bankrupt or, at the very least, being completely exhausted!

There are many wise reasons to avoid pregnancy at times. Severe illness, financial hardship, being overwhelmed by the number of children you already have, and many other life circumstances may mean that intentionally getting pregnant (or having sex during a woman's fertile time without contraception) is not wise. Scripture never says you must let God decide your family size as passive recipients; it does, however, frequently exhort believers to ask God for wisdom, receive wisdom from God, and exercise wisdom. There is no place for spiritual abuse that accuses believers of not trusting God; relying upon the wisdom and grace of the God who knows your life and your limits is a deep display of trust. Trusting God doesn't always look a certain way; as we join our lives to Christ's life, the encounter with God shapes our decisions, our circumstances, and our future.

While our biological systems for reproduction typically work as God intended, sin entered the world, bringing destruction and warping God's good gift of fertility. Throughout the Bible, many barren women cried out to God, knowing he held the power to make the barren fruitful.

Providence and Infertility

God's providence over birth is a frequent theme throughout the Old Testament, especially in relation to barrenness. In the Bible, there are several stories of barren women. God saw them, took notice of their suffering, and opened their wombs in miraculous ways.[4] God opened Sarah's womb in her old age, and she gave birth to Isaac. Isaac prayed for Rebekah, and the Lord answered with twins (Gen 25:21). God enabled Leah to conceive (29:31), and she acknowledged God's consideration of her as she gave birth to son after son. Rachel endured years of infertility alongside her very fertile sister, Leah, and God finally granted her two sons (Gen 30:22). Manoah's barren wife was visited by an angel and told she would bear a son—Samson (Judg 13:3). Hannah prayed for a son, and God opened her womb to conceive Samuel (1 Sam 1:10–20). Elizabeth gave birth to John the Baptist in her old age (Luke 1:7, 57). God's providence is obvious in the births of the prophets and of Jesus. Even before the conception of their children, many parents-to-be in the Bible were visited by angels who foretold the births of their children, who would be chosen servants of God.

But none of these women *remained* barren, as is the experience of many faithful believers today. The stories of these women in the Bible are included precisely because of God's intervention, and especially because of the importance of the children born to them: Isaac, Joseph, Samson, Samuel, John the Baptist—all major players in the redemptive story. One notable exception is Michal, wife of King David, and the cause of her sustained barrenness is unclear. It may be that David never slept with her again after she chided him for dancing before the ark of the covenant, or it may have been God's work to punish her (2 Sam 6:23).

Some falsely teach that since most faithful women in the Bible who were infertile eventually bore children, then a woman simply needs to have enough faith in God, or pray more, or (fill in the blank), and God will give her a baby. A quick Internet search about infertility in the Bible reveals several websites devoted to name-it-and-claim-it methods of achieving victory over infertility in faith. They teach that if you are infertile, it is because you do not believe God enough, do enough good works, or pray hard enough.

The problem with this approach is that it amounts to worship of a birth goddess. The ancient Babylonians and Canaanites surrounding Israel had fertility-inducing incantations, spells, prayers, and rituals to convince the fertility gods to grant offspring.[5] Mortals could manipulate these small gods to achieve pregnancy or secure good birth outcomes. No such incantations, rituals, or spells are found in the Bible. The worship of Yahweh was intended to be distinct from the worship of other Mesopotamian gods. Further, these teachings are outright denials of the gospel. No woman should be encouraged to try to earn God's favor so that she can get something from God. God blesses us freely through Christ—grace is a gift, not something earned by being holier. Rather than requiring women to insert the right pieces into a formula to get the desired outcome, the Bible encourages women to seek God in faith, to wrestle in prayer, and to trust his goodness and love. That can be much harder—though richer and more satisfying—than using God as a genie.

We do find models of faith and prayer in some of these women, and in the same women we also see God's hand of grace over sinners who didn't perform perfectly. Sarah didn't believe God when she was told she would bear a child in her old age. So she took matters into her own hands to provide an heir, giving her servant Hagar to Abraham to bear the promised child, saying, "The LORD has kept me from having children" (Gen 16:2). God fulfilled his promise anyway, providing a longed-for heir and beloved son whose name, Isaac ("he laughs"), echoed his mother's doubting laugh. The faith of Sarah is not a simple, black-and-white matter. It seems that she cycled in and out of faith and doubt, as we often find is true in our own experience. Hebrews 11 commends Sarah for her faith: "By faith even Sarah, who was past childbearing age, was enabled to bear children because she considered him faithful who had made the promise" (11:11). Sarah's laughter of doubt at God's promise turns to laughter of joy after childbirth: "Sarah said, 'God has brought me laughter, and everyone who hears about this will laugh with me.' And she added, 'Who would have said to Abraham that Sarah would nurse children? Yet I have borne him a son in his old age'" (Gen 21:6–7).

Rachel's faith is not straightforward either. Her literal sister wife, Leah, was not loved by their husband, Jacob. Scripture tells us that "when the LORD saw that Leah was not loved, he enabled her to conceive, but Rachel remained childless" (Gen 29:31). Rachel's agony over Leah's fruitfulness with their shared husband grew with each child Leah birthed. Rachel repeated Sarah's tactic of giving Jacob her servant to sleep with. The story of the birth of Jacob's 12 sons becomes a comical birth-race, as Leah and Rachel both give their servants to Jacob, who seems to be more than compliant. They even barter with mandrakes over who gets to sleep with Jacob (Gen 30:14–16). Finally, "God remembered Rachel; he listened to her and enabled her to conceive" (Gen 30:22). Rachel gave birth to Joseph and, later, Benjamin. But her methods are hardly worth copying! God gave unmerited grace to a sinner, not a woman whose faithfulness and prayer life were high above the norm.

Hannah's desperation and despair drove her toward God, not away from him, though Scripture says that "the LORD had closed her womb" (1 Sam 1:5–6). Her praying was so fervent and sincere that she was accused of being drunk in the temple! Hannah bargained with God, saying, "LORD Almighty, if you will only look on your servant's misery and remember me, and not forget your servant but give her a son, then I will give him to the LORD for all the days of his life, and no razor will ever be used on his head" (1:11). Hannah "was praying in her heart ... pouring out [her] soul to the LORD ... out of [her] great anguish and grief" (1:13–16). God granted Hannah's request in mercy, and she fulfilled her vow by bringing Samuel to the temple to serve the Lord there.

These women didn't secure their babies by doing the right things at the right time to make God grant them pregnancies. They were simply gifts of grace to ordinary women, some who had great faith and others who had very little. The point of the stories is not what the women did, but what *God* did. If we take the short view of these passages, we may only see that God filled the wombs of infertile women. This is something he still does today, but it isn't quite the point of these stories. God was breaking into the suffering of the world, interrupting the story line to shift the plot toward Jesus. Jacob continued the family line of Israel, which bears his God-given new name. Samuel was the prophet who anointed David as king over Israel, the forerunner of the coming King whose kingdom will never end. John the Baptist prepared the way for Jesus' life and ministry. These stories of God intervening in infertility ultimately lead us to Jesus, the promised child, who makes all things new.

What About Infertile Women?

Many women find it frustrating that the Bible does not have an exact model of a permanently barren woman for us to use as an example. Most of the women who are explicitly described as barren (save Michal) are eventually cured of their infertility. What about the women today who love Jesus but whose wombs remain empty? Proverbs 30:15–16 captures some of the emotion of infertility:

> There are three things that are never satisfied,
> four that never say, "Enough!":
> the grave, the barren womb,
> land, which is never satisfied with water,
> and fire, which never says, "Enough!"

This writer describes the never-ending need and longing of a barren womb to be filled. Women suffering in infertility don't need platitudes, Band-Aid solutions, or pity. We try to cheer up our friends who can't have babies by saying things like, "Hey, you can always adopt!" or "If you believe/pray/stay positive/relax, it will happen!" "Your time is coming!" "You can be a mentor to others and mother in that way!" Relentless optimism isn't enough. They need the gospel. It is here, at the foot of the cross and the entrance to the empty tomb, where honest questions can be brought to God and where sorrow will never be minimized. "Why is this happening to me? Do you even hear me? Do you even care?" When we ask these questions in light of all God has done out of love for us, it puts our grieving alongside his grief, rather than up against his unknown will. God, who sent his own beloved Son to die in our place, knows the grief. He sees you. He hears you.

Back in the garden of Eden, the entrance of death and sin into the very marrow of our bones meant that women would conceive and bear children in sorrow and grief. The whole system became tinged with danger and death. And while childbirth resoundingly depict God's love—with its hope, expectancy, and new life—it can also be a crossroads of life and death for some women and their babies. For many, the fall means that their wombs may remain empty. It's not the way it's supposed to be. In chapter 4, we discussed the in-breaking of God's kingdom in Christ, how wherever Jesus is, the will of God is done. The hungry are fed, the sick are healed, the dead rise—glimpses of heaven here on earth that point us to the coming day when death dies and *shalom* is restored. We are commanded to preach this kingdom, to pray for it to come, and to live as Jesus lived while we wait for it. We may lay our hands on infertile women and pray for healing and rejoice when God answers this prayer—he often does! But the kingdom is not fully here until Jesus returns. Loved ones still die, our bodies still get sick, and our wombs may stay empty.

We cannot place our hope and identity in whether our bodies are able to carry children to term. This is a false, unforgiving god that will never satisfy. God doesn't promise to cure all cases of infertility or chronic miscarriage or stillbirth. He promised us suffering would come, and it comes because the world is tainted by sin—and yet he has sent his Son to make it all new. Hoping only in God is a tough discipline. We cannot grow it in ourselves; God must nurture it in us.

It is easy to love a God who causes infertile women to conceive, but how do we feel about a God who, in his divine providence, closes wombs? This is something God clearly does in Scripture. In Genesis 20, Abraham lied to King Abimelek as they passed through Gerar, saying that Sarah was his sister.[6] God warned Abimelek in a dream not to touch Sarah, and when he returned her to Abraham, "Abraham prayed to God, and God healed Abimelek, his wife and his female slaves so they could have children again, for the LORD had kept all the women in Abimelek's household from conceiving because of Abraham's wife Sarah" (Gen 20:17–18). As we already saw, Scripture attributes the closed wombs of Rachel (Gen 30:2) and Hannah (1 Sam 1:5–6) to God's active influence.

Today, in the absence of a prophet to tell us why a woman cannot conceive, we may not ever know the full reason for each case of infertility. It may be the result of a sin, though accusing anyone of this is not helpful or right. It may be because of the fallenness and imperfection that racks our bodies. It could be for something God wants to teach her. It may be temporary. It may be her husband's infertility and not hers, though their burden is shared. Whatever the reason, we must wrestle with our feelings about a God who closes wombs. Do we assume he has done so because he loves those people less? Because they would be horrible parents? Because he enjoys our suffering or does not care or is far off and does not hear us? A closed womb can drive a woman to face her true view of God as she wrestles with him over it in honest prayer.

And of course, God does still open wombs. I can name many women who were told by doctors that they would never have children, and they went on to bear children anyway. My own mother had five children after receiving such a diagnosis—I am one of those children longed for, prayed for, and received. God delights in giving us the desires of our hearts. He delights in doing the impossible and showing his glory and power in weakness, frailty, and sickness. We can ask in faith, longing, anguish, and hope, knowing we are seen and heard. God's kingdom is that upside-down place where the marginalized are brought into the circle, where the previously cursed are called blessed, where despair gives way to hope:

> He raises the poor from the dust
> and lifts the needy from the ash heap;
> he seats them with princes,
> with the princes of his people.
> He settles the childless woman in her home
> as a happy mother of children (Psa 113:7–9).

But God is no small birth goddess who can be manipulated into giving us what we want. There is no formula, no "right" combination of words, no amount of optimism we can muster and label as faith, that can make God give us babies. If motherhood is the object of our faith, then we are worshiping a god that cannot satisfy. If the object of our faith is Jesus, then we have hope of being filled even if our arms stay empty forever. Because of his death, resurrection, and intercession for us at the right hand of God, we can come to his throne of grace freely, as we are, in our mess of emotions.

Children Are a Blessing

Children are described as a blessing or gift from God. "Children are a heritage from the LORD, offspring a reward from him" (Psa 127:3). Increasingly in our culture, children are seen as luxuries or accessories at best, inconveniences or curses at worst. Many parents note their frustration with the reactions of others to the gender of their second or third (or more!) baby if it's the same gender as the previous kids. "Three boys? Time for a girl!" There is an ingrained, consumerist idea in our culture about having a perfect set of children, as if they were bowls that matched with plates.

It can be difficult at times to remember that our children are blessings. When they are swaddled and quietly sleeping, when they nurse and snuggle, when they jump into our arms and obey quickly, we feel warm with affection and thank God for the blessing of children. But sometimes, the blessing feels hard. We may have spent years getting our lives settled before having children, only to find that these babes throw our well-ordered lives into chaos! When they develop a sassy attitude, or need to be walked back to bed for the hundredth time in an hour, or break our hearts as they fall into sin, the hardships and exhaustion of parenthood can make us forget that these little people *are* blessings.

God's providence in conception brings up difficult questions—and I can only offer more questions, not answers. What about children conceived as a result of rape? Are these children blessings or curses? When your teenage daughter shows you her pregnancy test, is this grandchild a blessing or a curse? When a woman discovers her baby has Down syndrome or cerebral palsy, is that baby still a blessing? When a child is diagnosed with autism spectrum disorder, is that child still a blessing? Unexpected disability can bring parents chronic mourning as they cycle in and out of grief for the "normal" life they will never have. They may be the recipients of pity, meaningless platitudes, or even accusations for doing something wrong during pregnancy to cause it.

That children are blessings brings the ethics of abortion and even some prenatal testing to the forefront. If children are blessings—complicated, multifaceted blessings, but blessings all the same—and not luxuries, then we cannot embark on a search for the "perfect" child. Prenatal testing for various disabilities and deformities can be helpful for preparing parents to care for the future needs of their children. But for many, a disability may bring the subject of termination to the table. Some may feel a deep sense of duty to prevent a life of suffering for the child and choose to abort. Does our desire to prevent pain go as far as to deny life to those who might experience suffering, though suffering is the norm for all humans?

The abortion debate needs fewer condemning, picket-lining, fire-bombing Christians, and more of the gospel. For some, pregnancy is truly terrifying in its life-altering power. God's providence over conception is not cause for us to wag our fingers in the faces of scared women and accuse them of scorning God's work.

God's providence over conception should stir our hearts to care deeply for vulnerable women who face difficult choices that will change lives.

The idea that God has formed this baby from conception and knows this child and his mother—every hair on their heads—should incite us to work toward making the blessing of children more visible to those who are confused. That God loved us at great cost to himself should lead us to adopt orphans and to gather in foster children who may desperately need this costly love. Rather than encouraging us to throw out our pregnant teenagers for not behaving, the gospel teaches us that we all are sinners—even if our sins may be less visible than theirs.

The gospel teaches us to forgive the sinner and seek reconciliation, as God has done for us. The gospel teaches self-sacrificial, costly love that seeks the best for others. Perhaps we should spend less time condemning women and instead work in the power of the Spirit to make life something a woman is realistically able to choose. God's involvement in bringing life to the world should help us see that God sees, knows, and loves each woman and her unborn child. As we lean into Jesus, we will find our hearts changed to match his own.

How God's Providence Impacts Our Souls

We may—falsely—believe that our circumstances show us whether God approves of us. We think that if God has chosen a difficult road for us in childbearing, then he must be displeased with us or be trying to make us learn something the hard way. If that same road is particularly easy, it must mean that God approves of us and perhaps has a better plan for our lives.

We hear this in subtle ways. When my friend walked away from a horrific car accident relatively unscathed, Christians proclaimed, "God wasn't finished with you yet! He has special plans for you!" I cannot help but wonder at the other dear ones who did not walk away from the same types of accidents. Do we mean to imply that God *was* finished with them? That he had no further special plans, that they were used up and cast off from God's favor? Of course we don't mean this. But it can feel like this is God's view of us when we face difficult things. The idea of God's providence can be difficult for those who have hard lives if they assume that good things happen when you have God's approval and that bad things happen when you are abandoned.

God's sovereignty goes hand-in-hand with God's love. His rule over our lives is for his glory and our good—though to us, it may not look as good as it *could* be for us. Who can tell why some suffer more than others? Who has wisdom to know why you and I were born where we were, why we're educated enough to read and write, and how we were each introduced to the gospel? Are we above those who remain illiterate, who are hungry and malnourished, and who will live and die without ever hearing the name of Jesus?

The providence of God is not the approval of God. I won't claim the wisdom to understand it, but I can choose to love God and hold fast to him whether I am receiving good gifts or deepest sufferings. The Heidelberg Catechism finishes its section on God's providence this way: "We can be patient in adversity, thankful in prosperity, and with a view to the future we can have a firm confidence in our faithful God and Father that no creature shall separate us from his love; for all creatures are so completely in his hand that without his will they cannot so much as move."[7]

Hebrews 11, the "Hall of Faith" passage, includes Sarah, whose womb God opened in his divine providence. But it also includes those who—though never outside of God's loving care—were tortured, imprisoned, stoned, sawed in half, persecuted, exiled, and afflicted (Heb 11:36–38). And the author continues:

> These were all commended for their faith, yet none of
> them received what had been promised, since God had
> planned something better for us so that only together
> with us would they be made perfect. Therefore, since
> we are surrounded by such a great cloud of witnesses,
> let us throw off everything that hinders and the sin that
> so easily entangles. And let us run with perseverance

the race marked out for us, fixing our eyes on Jesus, the
pioneer and perfecter of faith (Heb 11:39–12:2).

Like all of life, all of faith, childbirth can be unpredictable and scary.
We must fix our eyes on Jesus, running toward him even into suffering, knowing that we are never outside of God's loving care.

Unwanted infertility can be devastating for those facing it, but
like other hardships we face, God can use it to shape women. I fear
my words might ring insincere to women facing this reality; I myself have never experienced it, and my perspective needs widening by other women who can help me understand. A woman who
has walked through the desert of infertility or miscarriage will
be transformed when she walks with Jesus. She will have experienced longing and aching, staying up all night, praying and weeping. She will have to face her darkest envy as she faces yet another
pregnancy announcement not her own, another baby born to her
friends and family while her own arms remain empty. She will
have to come to terms with the insensitivity of those around her
to her plight, saying no to cynicism and anger and the pain of being misunderstood, and learn to respond with grace over time.

Romans 12:15 has good advice for those of us in the church
who face infertility and for those of us who bear child after child:
"Rejoice with those who rejoice, mourn with those who mourn."
As members of one body, we belong to one another. My joy is your
joy. My pain is your pain. Women who cling to Jesus will find they
have the emotional power to rejoice over another's good news,
though not in their own strength. It may take time and a lot of
prayer to overcome the trigger into grief that the sight of an infant
may cause. But as we press into Christ, we are transformed into his
image, and our hearts will begin to look like his. Even in pain, we
can rejoice in the good gifts God has given another without feeling
that he has done so by withholding blessing from us.

The Church's Care for All Women

For those of us who are in the thick of motherhood, we must take
care to remember those who weep and weep with them. While we

may not know the pain of infertility firsthand, God gives us grace to listen, understand, and notice when things are not okay. We can stop making suggestions to solve her problems and encourage her to persevere as she walks a hard road with Jesus. Mother's Day is a difficult holiday for many women who don't fit the mold. Churches want to honor mothers publicly but often unintentionally portray mothers as superior women with the hardest and best job in the world. As a whole, the church needs to find ways to honor mothers as a vital aspect of the body of Christ, while not diminishing the value of women who are not mothers. Harder still is the task of remaining sensitive to those whose motherhood status is difficult to define due to miscarriage, stillbirth, or death, and those whose infertility makes the discussion of motherhood very painful.

Of course, women are not the only ones to suffer from the pain of infertility. Infertility and miscarriage are not a woman's burden to bear alone but a grief shared by both her and her spouse. Women often lead the charge in discussing their feelings and hardships of an empty womb and grieving the loss of childbirth, breastfeeding, and mothering children. In Western culture, men are often expected to want children much less than women, and their grief at infertility may be minimized because of their gender. Even the Bible seems, at first glance, to support this, as infertility is generally assumed to be a female problem.

The community of God should help bear the burden of hardship and encourage one another to grow in Jesus. While some women bear the hardship of infertility, others need support as they give birth and raise children. Believers can provide encouragement for weary and fearful pregnant mothers who need prayer, meals, housework help, and hope. They may need skilled Christian doulas, midwives, and/or doctors who can help them embrace Jesus in the delivery room. They need help in the exhausting postpartum period so that they can rest, recover, and bond with their newborns. They can receive support from the body of Christ as they walk the shadows of postpartum depression, assured by the gospel of peace that there is light on the other side. They need the wisdom and mentorship of other mothers who have walked before them in the challenges of parenting. Childbirth and parenting work best within the family of God.

Whatever situation God, in his divine providence, has placed you in, he has provided the church to bear the burden with you. He has given us to one another for service in love, so that we may grow up in Christ together. "Speaking the truth in love, we will grow to become in every respect the mature body of him who is the head, that is, Christ. From him the whole body, joined and held together by every supporting ligament, grows and builds itself up in love, as each part does its work" (Eph 4:15–16).

Ultimately, as image-bearers of God, our identity is not in childbearing, but in Christ. Women who never become mothers—by choice or not—are not inferior, unfulfilled, or lacking. Women who are mothers are not merely successful uteruses, solely defined by their children and their role as mother. We cannot fully understand God's providence over our wombs and our lives. But we can trust his goodness no matter what our circumstances may be or become, because we know that in all things, he longs to make us like himself, and he is working for our good. May our eyes be attentive to God's work in our lives and in this world as we await the birth of the new heaven and new earth and of our bodies that will grieve no more.

Spiritual Disciplines for Chapter 6

In chapter 6, we examined the theology of God's providence as it relates to conception and childbirth. While we do not possess the wisdom to discern why God takes some people down one path and some on another, we must learn to trust God's love and care for us as we submit to his sovereignty over our lives. Learning this trust in the midst of hardship is often the hardest thing we can do, and engaging in spiritual disciplines over a long time can help us in that effort.

In this section, we'll discuss the disciplines of practicing God's presence and serving others. These disciplines help nurture trust and love for God in all circumstances as well as care and compassion for those with whom he has surrounded us.

Practicing God's Presence

In this chapter, we explored God's sovereignty over the womb and over the creation of children within their mothers. Losing sight of God's providential care in conception and childbirth can lead to the devaluing of both mother and child, as they are reduced to their potential usefulness or productivity. God's providence shows us that nothing is outside God's watchful and caring eye; no one is too small or insignificant to be noticed by God. The discipline of practicing God's presence helps us to live awake to God's work around us. Our senses are dulled by our inattentiveness to his involvement with us and our distraction by lesser things.

Seventeenth-century monk Brother Lawrence, in letters and conversations with Joseph de Beaufort, describes this discipline in the devotional classic *The Practice of the Presence of God*. Brother Lawrence's main duty during the time he wrote these letters was scrubbing kitchen pots, which he detested, as well as other menial chores. When he began to practice intentional awareness of God's presence with him, he found that his mundane tasks were transformed into beautiful acts of love and adoration to God. He spoke simply with God, asking for help when he needed it or confessing sin when necessary. Recalling a conversation with Brother Lawrence, de Beaufort writes, "All we have to do is recognize God as being intimately present within us. Then we may speak directly to Him every time we need to ask for help, to know His will in moments of uncertainty, and to do whatever He wants us to do in a way that pleases Him. We should offer our work to Him before we begin and thank Him afterward for the privilege of having done it for His sake. This continuous conversation should also include praising and loving God incessantly for His infinite goodness and perfection."[8]

This discipline of divine attentiveness has been, for me, the most important discipline I've developed as I've walked with God through pregnancy, childbirth, and motherhood. Abiding in God's presence energizes me for the work I do, and it brings meaning and sanctity to humble acts. For me, this quiet communion with God is when I can appreciate that God is knitting *this* child together in *my* womb. It is in God's presence where I can find peace from his loving-kindness and mercy as I groan in labor. It is only when I am aware of his nearness to me in the soapsuds, the endless diapers, the correction of my children, and the mountains of unfinished laundry that I can find meaning in the mundane tasks that fill my days. If I begin to feel that he doesn't care about any of this, that he is far away with people of higher importance for his kingdom purposes, then I have lost sight of the providential care of our eminent God.

Living with eyes wide open to God draws us into his love and away from the cynicism and hopelessness that comes when we perceive God as uncaring, distant, and deistic. We serve a living, resurrected Savior who longs to abide with us—he even stands at the door and knocks (Rev 3:20).[9] Through this intentional remaining in his presence, we learn what it is to abide in Christ and to "pray continually" (1 Thess 5:17). We have access to God's presence whether our wombs are fruitful or barren, whether we have easy pregnancies or endure tragedy upon tragedy. We can rest in God's love, knowing that we do not suffer apart from his providential care and that suffering does not mean he disapproves of us. Practicing God's presence in labor can enable us to anchor ourselves to Christ, trusting in him through each contraction and banishing fear in his name. We can bask in his pleasure as we hold our newborns, worshiping our wonderful creator as we count tee-ny fingers and toes. In doing so, we do not bring God into our lives, but notice how he is already there. And as we press further into his heart, we begin to see our neighbors around us with the love God has for them. This leads us to the discipline of service.

Service

Our natural human tendency is to serve ourselves first, and with whatever spare energy we happen to have left over, we may serve others (though often, only if we will get recognition for it). The discipline of service is an attempt to follow the example and commands of Jesus by crucifying our selfish desires and putting others before our own needs and ambitions. The discipline of service often goes hand-in-hand with secrecy—not to be deceptive but to ward off our desire for recognition when we serve others. Our hearts cry out to be rewarded and noticed by others, but the discipline of service is done for the pleasure of God alone and for the good of others.

Of course, service may become second nature to mothers, as they continually have to put the needs of their children above their own. How many of us have gone until mid-afternoon only to re-alize we had fed our kids two meals and cleaned up after them but forgot to eat ourselves? Outward acts of service may be done with-out the inward heart of service, though. The martyrdom complex that is so tempting for many moms may undermine our works of service with a begrudging heart full of self-pity. This is hardly the spirit of the discipline of service!

We serve because we have the fullness of Jesus, who served us in humility and self-sacrificing love. Jesus told his recognition-hungry disciples, "Whoever wants to become great among you must be your servant, and whoever wants to be first must be slave of all. For even the Son of Man did not come to be served, but to serve, and to give his life as a ransom for many" (Mark 10:43-45). The night before Jesus' ultimate sacrificial act, he demonstrated his greatness by washing the nasty feet of his disciples—the job they were all trying to avoid! Jesus tells them, and us:

> Now that I, your Lord and Teacher, have washed your feet, you also should wash one another's feet. I have set you an example that you should do as I have done for you. Very truly I tell you, no servant is greater than his master, nor is a messenger greater than the one who sent him. Now that you know these things, you will be blessed if you do them (John 13:14-17).

The discipline of service is often difficult because of the insignificance of the tasks we are drawn into. Books abound on Christian leadership, casting grand visions, catalyzing movements, and doing great things for God. But sometimes the most obedient thing we can do is set aside any position we've gained, pull out a towel, and scrub the toes of a bunch of nobodies. This, according to Jesus, is the kind of thing that will probably get no attention from the world, yet somehow it is the definition of greatness in his kingdom. Those who want to become great must become servants. Acts of service, however small, done in the presence of God, free us from the need for others' approval and from our egos' need for greatness and significance.

The realities and complexities of childbirth, infertility, and parenthood are a wonderful context for developing servanthood within families and within the church. In these aspects of our lives we need one another, and often the needs we have are so mundane that they can be overlooked. We should not demand that others serve us, but we should be willing to give time and effort to care for one another in various ways. Postpartum depression rates are on the rise in the United States and in many Western countries where support for new mothers in the postpartum period is minimal. Women are expected to resume household duties within days after birth, as their husbands rarely are granted paternity leave. And the prevalence of the nuclear family as the norm means that new mothers may be far away from family support structures. Most U.S. women receive only six weeks of maternity leave if they continue their employment, and they may not be paid for this time. The overwhelming task of caring for a newborn on very little sleep may be compounded by breastfeeding issues, housecleaning, cooking, and caring for older children. Feeling isolated and overwhelmed can lead a new mother into despair and depression. The church has the privilege of serving these mothers in various practical ways.

Motherhood can also be a fertile field in which the seeds of service are sown and the graces of humility and meekness are harvested. It can be difficult to serve young children for years without reward. Many mothers trade big dreams for feelings of smallness as they focus on raising their children. Motherhood can be a bitter task, or it can be redeemed before the God of grace as a constant washing of feet as we surrender these tasks to him in love. As we give ourselves in service to our neighbors and families, we do so knowing that God sees, cares, and considers these tiny acts as great in his kingdom.

Exercises for Practicing God's Presence and Service

1. As you do the mundane tasks of your day, offer up the things you are doing to God as worship. Talk with him about what you are doing, where your heart is at the moment, whatever comes to mind. His presence is always with you; be attentive to him. Do this as often as you remember—try to practice his presence for a whole day as you grow in this discipline.

2. Reflect on what Joseph de Beaufort says of Brother Lawrence's discipline: "Although he once had a great dislike for kitchen work, he developed quite a facility for doing it over the fifteen years he was there. He attributed this to his doing everything for the love of God, asking as often as possible for grace to do his work. ... He would be willing to work anywhere, always rejoicing at being able to do little things for the love of God."[10]

Consider the ways you can implement this love for God and a sense of his presence as you perform daily tasks and serve others.

3. With a group of both men and women from your church, brainstorm ways you could work together to meet the needs of new mothers, women who are suffering from miscarriage or infertility, and those who are pregnant. How will you lovingly serve those outside the church? Will they have to come to you, or could you go to them? Are there ways your fellowship can consider the needs of potentially abortive mothers, couples who need help in the adoption process, or those who need support and encouragement in caring for foster children?

4. Consider the ways you serve others already. Do you do these acts of service for the good of others and in the love of God, or do you do them begrudgingly or because you have to? Think of three ways you can serve others this week, especially in undesirable or mundane tasks. Try to keep the act secret if you can, and do it in an attitude of love and service to God.

5. Search the Scriptures for commandments, teachings, and stories about service, especially in the New Testament. Make notes on all that you learn, and commit yourself to obedience in whatever the Lord shows you.

6. If you have young children, focus a day on doing all of your mundane parenting acts (changing diapers, making meals, feeding, giving baths, time-outs) as both acts of worship to God and acts of service to your little people. Watch for the moments when you get frustrated, bored, tired, or sad, and acknowledge those emotions. What is at the root of them? Bitterness over a lost dream? Boredom? Selfishness? Lack of sleep? Pray these things back to God and ask for what you need in that moment.

ACKNOWLEDGMENTS

I've finished this book, and I'm in awe that it actually happened. I began writing this in the trenches of young motherhood: My sons were 3 and 1, and I was pregnant with my daughter. By the time I finished, we had moved three times within the United States, and then one move to the Middle East and began Arabic studies. I say this not to put myself on a pedestal of incredible industry; quite the contrary, I see this accomplishment as proof of God's miraculous grace. As I stand and look back, I see a great "cloud of witnesses" that shaped the many ideas that have developed into this book, and many hundreds of people who prayed, supported, told their stories, babysat, and contributed in ways I cannot even recall.

Thank you, Brady, for partnering with me in this life, for our three children, for being the best husband, labor coach, pregnancy craving-fulfiller, and father to our kids. Thanks for joyfully embracing your new role as "the man who weirdly knows too much about childbirth." It's an honor to be by your side. I love you.

Thank you, dear Latha, for helping care for my children while I finished this book! You are a Godsend.

So many prayers of faithful saints were behind me, far too many to name—especially the people of The Neighborhood Church in Garland, Texas, and the many precious friends we've gathered up in our nomadic life. Thank you to my friends here in the desert, who encouraged me to persevere through culture shock and grief and prayed over me as I finished this manuscript.

Special thanks to the hundreds of beautiful women who shared their birth and infertility stories with me, including Katie Mahfouz, Jolin Housewright, Laurie Hudgins, Libby Baker, Michelle Powell, Rachael Scrobot, Paige Greenway, Maria LaMarche, Britney Baer,

Amy Cowen, Beth Raven, Emily Feicht, Becca Owens, and Kelsey Clardy. You've all developed my perspective and changed me forever. Holly Hooten, thank you for giving over your story to God for his glory, and all the contributions you made to this book. They are more than you know. Thank you to my in-laws, Rick and Beth Smith, and Kris Hooten, for your loving support for this project and for welcoming me into your family right from the start.

I'm grateful to Childbirth International, where I received training and certification as a childbirth educator and a doula in the process of writing this book. I'm especially thankful for my trainer, Yonit Kasten, who gave me insightful feedback and rounded out my perspective on birth and supporting women through childbirth. The midwives at Lovers Lane Birth Center in Richardson, Texas, attended my third birth with joy and calmness, and shaped the way I approach birth. Thanks so much, Kristine, Dinah, and Brenda.

Thanks to Dr. J. Scott Duvall, my spiritual formation professor, boss, pastor, and mentor at Ouachita Baptist University. A lot of the ideas here began as seeds planted during conversations in your classroom and office. And Tracey Knight, whose mothering of me while I slowly lost my own mother shaped many of my ideas about God as a parent.

I'm so grateful to the folks at Faithlife who gave me some of my first professional writing opportunities and guided me through this process to publication, especially John Barry, Rebecca Van Noord, Brannon Ellis, Justin Marr, and Abigail Stocker. A huge thank you to my editor Jennifer Stair, who made me sound smarter than I am. The mistakes that remain are my own.

And thank you, Jesus, for your ineffable love, your presence among us, and your transformation of us into your likeness. May the words of my mouth and the meditations of my heart be pleasing in your sight, my rock and my redeemer.

BIBLIOGRAPHY

Albers, L., Anderson, D., and L. Cragin. "The relationship of ambulation in labour to operative delivery." *Journal of Nurse Midwifery* 42, no.1 (1997): 4–8.

Almendrala, Anna. "U.S. C-Section Rate is Double What WHO Recommends." *Huffington Post.* Last modified April 16, 2015. Accessed September 2, 2015. http://www.huffingtonpost. com/2015/04/14/c-section-rate-recommendation_n_7058954.html.

Bailey, Kenneth. *Jesus Through Middle Eastern Eyes.* Downers Grove, IL: InterVarsity Press, 2008. Kindle.

Bock, Darrell L. *Luke.* NIV Application Commentary. Grand Rapids: Zondervan, 1998.

Brother Lawrence. *The Practice of the Presence of God.* New Kensington, PA: Whitaker House, 1982.

Buckley, Sarah J. *Hormonal Physiology of Childbearing: Evidence and Implications for Women, Babies, and Maternity Care.* Washington, D.C.: Childbirth Connection Programs, National Partnership for Women & Families, 2015. Accessed April 19, 2016. http://transform.childbirth-connection.org/reports/physiology/.

———. *Pain in Labour: Your Hormones Are Your Helpers.* Sarah Buckley. 2005. Accessed April 19, 2016. http://sarahbuckley.com/ pain-in-labour-your-hormones-are-your-helpers.

Burge, Gary M. *John.* NIV Application Commentary. Grand Rapids: Zondervan, 2000.

California Health and Human Services. "Utilization Rates for Selected Medical Procedures." CHHS Open Data. Last modified March 12, 2015. Accessed September 2, 2015. https://chhs.data.ca.gov/ Healthcare/Utilization-Rates-for-Selected-Medical-Procedures-/ wum2-k452?.

Cassidy, Tina. *Birth: The Surprising History of How We Are Born.* New York: Grove Press, 2006.

Caughey, A. B., et al. "Maternal and Neonatal Outcomes of Elective Induction of Labor." *Agency for Healthcare Research and Quality (US) Evidence Reports/Technology Assessments* 176 (March 2009). Accessed September 2, 2015. http://www.ncbi.nlm.nih.gov/books/NBK38683/.

Centers for Disease Control and Prevention. "Births—Method of Delivery." Centers for Disease Control and Prevention Faststats. Last modified July 17, 2015. Accessed September 2, 2015. http://www.cdc.gov/nchs/fastats/delivery.htm.

Clark, John C., and Marcus Peter Johnson. *The Incarnation of God: The Mystery of the Gospel as the Foundation of Evangelical Theology.* Wheaton: Crossway, 2015.

Colijn, Brenda B. *Images of Salvation in the New Testament.* Downers Grove, IL: InterVarsity Press, 2010.

Dick-Read, Grantly. *Childbirth Without Fear: The Principles and Practice of Natural Childbirth.* London: Pinter & Martin, 2005.

Dye, John H. *Illustrated Edition of Painless Childbirth: Healthy Mothers and Healthy Children.* 19th Edition. Buffalo, NY: Dr. J. H. Dye Medical Institute, 1912. Accessed September 2, 2015. http://archive.org/details/illustratededitioodyej.

Foster, Richard J. *Celebration of Discipline: The Path to Spiritual Growth.* 20th Anniversary ed. New York: Harper Collins, 1998.

———. *Sanctuary of the Soul: Journey into Meditative Prayer.* Downers Grove, IL: InterVarsity Press, 2011.

Gaskin, Ina May. *Birth Matters: A Midwife's Manifesta.* New York: Seven Stories Press, 2011.

———. *Ina May's Guide to Childbirth.* New York: Bantam Books, 2003.

———. "Maternal Death in the United States: A Problem Solved or a Problem Ignored?" *The Journal of Perinatal Education* 17, no. 2 (2008): 9–13.

Glancy, Jennifer. *Corporal Knowledge: Early Christian Bodies.* Oxford: Oxford University Press, 2010.

Goetzl, L. M. "Obstetric Analgesia and Anesthesia." *ACOG Practice Bulletin, Clinical Management Guidelines for Obstetrician-Gynecologists* 100, no. 36 (July 2002): 177–91.

Goodfellow, C. F., et al. "Oxytocin Deficiency at Delivery with Epidural Analgesia." *British Journal of Obstetric Gynaecology* 90, no. 3 (1983): 214–19.

Hamilton, Victor P. *The Book of Genesis: Chapters 1–17*. The New
International Commentary on the Old Testament. Grand Rapids:
Eerdmans, 1990.

Hammer, Margaret. *Giving Birth: Reclaiming Biblical Metaphor for Pastoral
Practice*. Louisville, KY: Westminster John Knox Press, 1994.

Harrison, V. E. F. "Male and Female in Cappadocian Theology." *Journal of
Theological Studies* 41, no.2, (Oct 1990): 441–71.

Heidelberg Catechism. "Lord's Day 10." Canadian Reformed Theological
Seminary. Accessed March 3, 2015. http://www.heidelberg-catechism.
com/en/lords-days/10.html.

Hood, Jason B. *Imitating God in Christ: Recapturing a Biblical Pattern*.
Downers Grove, IL: InterVarsity Press, 2013.

Kapic, Kelly M., and Justin Borger. *God So Loved, He Gave: Entering the
Movement of Divine Generosity*. Grand Rapids: Zondervan, 2010.

Kitzinger, Sheila. "Obstetric Metaphors and Marketing." *BIRTH: Issues in
Perinatal Care* 26, no. 1 (Mar 1999).

———. *Rediscovering Birth*. Revised Edition. London: Pinter & Martin,
2011. Kindle.

Labberton, Mark. *The Dangerous Act of Worship: Living God's Call to Justice*.
Downers Grove, IL: InterVarsity Press, 2007. Kindle.

Leap, Nicky. "No Pain Without Gain!" Birth International. Accessed
March 4, 2015. http://www.birthinternational.com/articles/
midwifery/81-no-gain-without-pain.

Lurie, S. "Euphemia Maclean, Agnes Sampson and Pain Relief during Labor
in 16th Century Edinburgh." *Anaesthesia* 59, no. 8 (2004): 834–35.

Mathews, Kenneth A. *Genesis 1-11:26*. New American Commentary. Nashville:
Broadman & Holman, 1996.

Mathews, T. J., and Marian F. MacDorman. "Infant Mortality Statistics from
the 2010 Period Linked Birth/Infant Death Data Set." *Centers for
Disease Control and Prevention National Vital Statistics Reports* 62, no.8
(December 18, 2013): 1–16. Accessed September 2, 2015. http://www.
cdc.gov/nchs/data/nvsr/nvsr62/nvsr62_08.pdf.

Morris, Leon. *The Gospel According to John*. New International Commentary
on the New Testament. Grand Rapids: Eerdmans, 1995.

Nouwen, Henri. *The Inner Voice of Love*. New York: Image, 1998.

Piper, John. "The Frank and Manly Mr. Ryle: The Value of a Masculine
Ministry." Desiring God. Last modified January 31, 2012. Accessed
November 20, 2013. http://www.desiringgod.org/resource-library/

biographies/the-frank-and-manly-mr-ryle-the-value-of-a-masculine-ministry.

Plantinga, Cornelius, Jr. *Not the Way It's Supposed to Be: A Breviary of Sin.* Grand Rapids: Eerdmans, 1995.

Rienstra, Debra. *Great With Child: On Becoming a Mother.* La Porte, IN: WordFarm, 2008. Kindle.

Safe Motherhood Quilt Project. http://rememberthemothers.org.

Selo-Ojeme, D., C. Rogers, A. Mohanty, N. Zaidi, R. Villar, and P. Shangaris. "Is induced labour in the nullipara associated with more maternal and perinatal morbidity?" *Archives of Gynecology and Obstetrics* 284, no. 2 (August 2011): 337–41. Print.

Smith, James Bryan. *The Good and Beautiful God: Falling in Love with the God Jesus Knows.* Downers Grove, IL: InterVarsity Press, 2009.

Spong, Catherine Y., et al. "Preventing the First Cesarean Delivery: Summary of a Joint Eunice Kennedy Shriver National Institute of Child Health and Human Development, Society for Maternal-Fetal Medicine, and American College of Obstetricians and Gynecologists Workshop." *Obstetrics and Gynecology* 120, no. 5 (2012): 1181–93. Print.

Stol, M. *Birth in Babylonia and the Bible: Its Mediterranean Setting.* Cuneiform Monographs 14. Ed. T. Abusch, et al. Groningen: Styx, 2000.

Stott, John. *Guard the Truth: The Message of 1 Timothy and Titus.* Downers Grove, IL: InterVarsity Press, 1996.

Thatcher, Adrian. *God, Sex, and Gender.* West Sussex, UK: Wiley-Blackwell, 2011.

Towner, Philip H. *The Letters to Timothy and Titus.* New International Commentary on the New Testament. Grand Rapids: Eerdmans, 2006.

Trible, Phyllis. *God and the Rhetoric of Sexuality.* Overtures to Biblical Theology. Philadelphia: Fortress Press, 1978. Kindle.

Voskamp, Ann. *One Thousand Gifts: A Dare to Live Fully Right Where You Are.* Grand Rapids: Zondervan, 2010.

Walton, John H. *Genesis.* The NIV Application Commentary. Grand Rapids: Zondervan, 2001.

Ward, Benedicta, ed. *Prayers and Meditations of St. Anselm with the Proslogion.* Hardmondsworth: Penguin Classics, 1979.

Wenham, Gordon J. *Genesis 1–15.* Word Biblical Commentary. Waco: Word Books, 1987.

Wesley, Charles. "Glory Be to God on High (Wesley 2)." *The Cyber Hymnal.* Accessed March 31, 2016. http://www.hymntime.com/tch/htm/g/b/g/gbgohigh.htm.

World Bank. "Maternal Mortality Ratio (modeled estimate, per 100,000 live births)." Trends in Maternal Mortality, 1990–2013. Last modified 2014. Accessed September 2, 2015. http://data.worldbank.org/indicator/SH.STA.MMRT

World Health Organization. "Caesarean sections should only be performed when medically necessary." WHO Media Center. Last modified April 10, 2015. Accessed September 2, 2015. http://www.who.int/mediacentre/news/releases/2015/caesarean-sections/en/.

———. "Female Genital Mutilation." WHO Media Center. Last modified February 2016. Accessed February 27, 2016. http://www.who.int/mediacentre/factsheets/fs241/en/.

———. "Maternal Mortality." WHO Media Center. Last modified May 2014. Accessed March 4, 2015. http://www.who.int/mediacentre/factsheets/fs348/en/.

Introduction: A Biblical Perspective of Childbirth

1. John Piper, "The Frank and Manly Mr. Ryle: The Value of a Masculine Ministry," Desiring God, last modified January 31, 2012, accessed November 20, 2013, http://www.desiringgod.org/resource-library/biographies/the-frank-and-manly-mr-ryle-the-value-of-a-masculine-ministry.
2. If it helps, we do know Jesus was swaddled. So there's that.

Chapter 1: Eve's Curse and Our Narrative of God

1. James Bryan Smith, *The Good and Beautiful God* (Downers Grove, IL: InterVarsity Press, 2009), 31.
2. S. Lurie, "Euphemia Maclean, Agnes Sampson and Pain Relief during Labor in 16th Century Edinburgh," *Anaesthesia* 59, no. 8 (2004): 834.
3. Tina Cassidy, *Birth: The Surprising History of How We Are Born* (New York: Grove Press, 2006), 85.
4. John H. Dye, *Illustrated Edition of Painless Childbirth: Healthy Mothers and Healthy Children*, 19th Edition (Buffalo, NY: Dr. J. H. Dye Medical Institute, 1912), accessed September 2, 2015, http://archive.org/details/illustratededitioodyej.
5. Ina May Gaskin, *Ina May's Guide to Childbirth* (New York: Bantam Books 2003), 5–125.
6. Cornelius Plantinga, Jr., *Not the Way It's Supposed to Be: A Breviary of Sin* (Grand Rapids: Eerdmans, 1995), 10.
7. John H. Walton, *Genesis*, The NIV Application Commentary (Grand Rapids: Zondervan, 2001), 231.
8. Victor P. Hamilton, *The Book of Genesis: Chapters 1–17*, The New International Commentary on the Old Testament (Grand Rapids: Eerdmans, 1990), 192.
9. Walton, *Genesis*, 229.

10. Gordon J. Wenham, *Genesis 1–15*, Word Biblical Commentary (Waco: Word Books, 1987), 80.

11. Kenneth A. Mathews, *Genesis 1–11:26*, New American Commentary (Nashville: Broadman & Holman, 1996), 243.

12. Walton, *Genesis*, 227.

13. Grantly Dick-Read, *Childbirth Without Fear: The Principles and Practice of Natural Childbirth* (London: Pinter & Martin, 2005), 18–19.

14. Gaskin, *Ina May's Guide to Childbirth*, 135–41.

15. Hamilton, *Genesis*, 195.

16. Of course, corrupt practices and injustice are at play here, too, also a result of the broken *shalom* with our creator.

17. Mathews, *Genesis*, 248.

18. Philip H. Towner, *The Letters to Timothy and Titus*, New International Commentary on the New Testament (Grand Rapids: Eerdmans, 2006), 196.

19. Ibid., 235.

20. John Stott, *Guard the Truth: The Message of 1 Timothy and Titus* (Downers Grove, IL: InterVarsity Press, 1996), 87. The Greek literally reads "the childbearing."

21. Richard Foster, *Sanctuary of the Soul: Journey into Meditative Prayer* (Downers Grove, IL: InterVarsity, 2011), 12.

Chapter 2: Image-Bearers of the God Who Gives Birth

1. Kelly M. Kapic and Justin Borger, *God So Loved, He Gave: Entering the Movement of Divine Generosity* (Grand Rapids: Zondervan, 2010), 24; referencing Calvin, *Institutes of the Christian Religion*, The Library of Christian Classics (Philadelphia: Westminster, 1960), 1.255.

2. Male gods were also worshiped and given offerings to a lesser extent, as the sex lives of gods and goddesses together greatly affected the natural world.

3. Sheila Kitzinger, *Rediscovering Birth*, revised edition (London: Pinter & Martin, 2011), Kindle ebook, chap. 3.

4. Ina May Gaskin, *Birth Matters: A Midwife's Manifesta* (New York: Seven Stories Press, 2011), 55.

5. Margaret Hammer, *Giving Birth: Reclaiming Biblical Metaphor for Pastoral Practice* (Louisville, KY: Westminster John Knox Press, 1994), 2–3.

6. Adrian Thatcher, *God, Sex, and Gender* (West Sussex, UK: Wiley-Blackwell: 2011), 119.

7. Ibid., 119.

8. Hammer, *Giving Birth*, 45.

9. It may be noted here that millions of Muslims think Christians believe God had sex with Mary to have Jesus.

10. V. E. F. Harrison, "Male and Female in Cappadocian Theology," *Journal of Theological Studies* 41, no. 2 (Oct 1990), 441–71.

11. Benedicta Ward, ed., *Prayers and Meditations of St. Anselm with the Proslogion* (Hardmondsworth: Penguin Classics, 1979), 358.

12. Jason B. Hood, *Imitating God in Christ: Recapturing a Biblical Pattern* (Downers Grove, IL: InterVarsity Press, 2013).

13. Hammer, *Giving Birth*, 31.

14. Thanks to J. Scott Duvall for blending the theologies of God's greatness and goodness with this simple childhood prayer in a Spiritual Formation lecture. It was a simple thing that continues to shape my view of God.

15. Mark Labberton, *The Dangerous Act of Worship: Living God's Call to Justice* (Downers Grove, IL: InterVarsity Press, 2007), Kindle ebook, chap. 1.

Chapter 3: God's Involvement in the Incarnation and Childbirth

1. "Glory Be to God on High (Wesley 2)," Charles Wesley, *The Cyber Hymnal*, accessed March 31, 2016, http://www.hymntime.com/tch/htm/g/b/g/gbg-ohigh.htm.

2. Leon Morris, *The Gospel According to John*, New International Commentary on the New Testament (Grand Rapids: Eerdmans, 1995), 91–93.

3. Darrell Bock notes that Galilee, and especially the town of Nazareth within Galilee, was a humble agrarian village often looked down upon, and certainly not where God would be expected to make such a significant announcement. Darrell Bock, *Luke*, NIV Application Commentary (Grand Rapids: Zondervan, 1998), 56.

4. John C. Clark and Marcus Peter Johnson, *The Incarnation of God: The Mystery of the Gospel as the Foundation of Evangelical Theology* (Wheaton: Crossway, 2015), 103.

5. Ibid., 133.

6. Ibid., 143.

7. Tertullian, *Against Marcion*, book 3, chapter 11.

8. Jennifer Glancy, *Corporal Knowledge: Early Christian Bodies* (Oxford: Oxford University Press, 2010) 81–136.

9. Ibid., 81.

10. To his credit as a godly man, Joseph planned to quietly divorce her, to spare her the shame, until the angel commanded him otherwise in a dream.

11. Kenneth Bailey, *Jesus Through Middle Eastern Eyes* (Downers Grove, IL: InterVarsity Press, 2008), Kindle ebook, chap. 4.

12. The Fear-Tension-Pain cycle was first made famous by Dr. Grantly Dick-Read's book *Childbirth Without Fear: The Principles and Practice of Natural Childbirth*, originally published in 1942. Many childbirth educators and birth writers touch on the subject; one good, more modern read is Dr. Sarah J. Buckley's *Hormonal Physiology of Childbearing*, available to read online: http://transform.childbirthconnection.org/reports/physiology/

13. Richard Foster, *Celebration of Discipline*, 20th Anniversary Edition (New York: Harper Collins, 1998), 193.

14. Ann Voskamp, *One Thousand Gifts: A Dare to Live Fully Right Where You Are* (Grand Rapids: Zondervan, 2010).

Chapter 4: Childbirth as a Picture of the Kingdom of God

1. World Bank, "Maternal Mortality Ratio (modeled estimate, per 100,000 live births)," Trends in Maternal Mortality, 1990–2013, last modified 2014, accessed September 2, 2015, http://data.worldbank.org/indicator/SH.STA. MMRT. These statistics are difficult to get accuracy on because of the lack of mandatory reporting by hospitals on maternal mortality, and lack of routine autopsies on mothers who die in childbirth. The United States ranks lowest of the wealthiest countries in the world, at 28 deaths per 100,000 live births. Many countries have less than 10 deaths per 100,000 live births.

2. Ina May Gaskin, "Maternal Death in the United States: A Problem Solved or a Problem Ignored?" *The Journal of Perinatal Education* 17, no. 2 (2008): 9–13. Also see her Safe Motherhood Quilt Project at http://rememberthemothers.org.

3. Centers for Disease Control and Prevention, "Births—Method of Delivery," Centers for Disease Control and Prevention Faststats, last modified July 17, 2015, accessed September 2, 2015, http://www.cdc.gov/nchs/fastats/delivery.htm.

4. World Health Organization, "Caesarean sections should only be performed when medically necessary," WHO Media Center, last modified April 10, 2015, accessed September 2, 2015, http://www.who.int/mediacentre/news/releases/2015/caesarean-sections/en/.

5. California Health and Human Services, "Utilization Rates for Selected Medical Procedures," CHHS Open Data, last modified March 12, 2015, accessed September 2, 2015, https://chhs.data.ca.gov/Healthcare/Utilization-Rates-for-Selected-Medical-Procedures-/wum2-k452?.

6. Anna Almendrala, "U.S. C-Section Rate is Double What WHO Recommends," Huffington Post, last modified April 16, 2015, accessed September 2, 2015, http://www.huffingtonpost.com/2015/04/14/c-section-rate-recommendation_n_7058954.html.

7. The expectation of one centimeter of cervical dilation per hour comes from an old model called the Friedman Curve, established in 1955. Researchers have since shown that Friedman's methods can't be applied to normal childbirth, since about 90 percent of his patients were sedated with Twilight Sleep drugs. In 2012, the American College of Obstetricians and Gynecologists, Eunice Kennedy Shriver National Institute of Child Health and Human Development, and the Society for Maternal-Fetal Medicine held a joint workshop to create a plan to reduce the number of cesarean sections in first-time mothers. One of the major conclusions of this workshop was to increase the amount of time deemed "acceptable" for cervical dilation, since evidence widely suggests that Friedman's Curve was flawed, and that many women take much more time to dilate than his sigmoid graph depicted.

For more on this workshop, see Catherine Y. Spong, et al., "Preventing the First Cesarean Delivery: Summary of a Joint Eunice Kennedy Shriver National Institute of Child Health and Human Development, Society for Maternal-Fetal Medicine, and American College of Obstetricians and Gynecologists Workshop," *Obstetrics and Gynecology* 120, no. 5 (2012): 1181–93. Print. (Also available online at http://www.ncbi.nlm.nih.gov/pmc/articles/PMC3548444. Accessed April 17, 2016.)

8. A. B. Caughey, et al., "Maternal and Neonatal Outcomes of Elective Induction of Labor," *Agency for Healthcare Research and Quality (US) Evidence Reports/Technology Assessments* 176, accessed September 2, 2015, http://www.ncbi.nlm.nih.gov/booksNBK38683/.

9. D. Selo-Ojeme, C. Rogers, A. Mohanty, N. Zaidi, R. Villar, and P. Shangaris, "Is induced labour in the nullipara associated with more maternal and perinatal morbidity?," *Archives of Gynecology and Obstetrics* 284, no. 2 (August 2011): 337–41.

Results: "Compared to those in spontaneous labor, women who had induction of labor were three times more likely to have a caesarean delivery. Women who had induction of labour were 2.2 times more likely to have oxytocin augmentation, 3.6 times more likely to have epidural anesthesia, 1.7 times more likely to have uterine hyper stimulation, 2 times more likely to have a suspicious foetal heart rate trace, 4.1 times more likely to have blood loss over 500 ml, and 2.9 times more likely to stay in hospital beyond 5 days. Babies born to mothers who had induction of labour were significantly more likely to have an Apgar score of <5 at 5 min and an arterial cord pH of <7.0."

10. L. Albers, D. Anderson, and L. Cragin, "The relationship of ambulation in labour to operative delivery," *Journal of Nurse Midwifery* 42, no. 1 (1997): 4–8.

11. T. J. Mathews and Marian F. MacDorman, "Infant Mortality Statistics from the 2010 Period Linked Birth/Infant Death Data Set," *Centers for Disease Control and Prevention National Vital Statistics Reports* 62, no. 8 (December 18, 2013): 1–16, accessed September 2, 2015, http://www.cdc.gov/nchs/data/nvsr/nvsr62/nvsr62_08.pdf. Findings: The U.S. infant mortality rate was 6.14 infant deaths per 1,000 live births in 2010—11.46 per 1,000 for black mothers, 5.18 for white mothers.

12. World Health Organization, "Maternal Mortality," WHO Media Center, last modified May 2014, accessed March 4, 2015, http://www.who.int/mediacentre/factsheets/fs348/en/.

13. Not her real name.

14. World Health Organization, "Female Genital Mutilation," WHO Media Center, last modified Feb 2016, accessed February 27, 2016, http://www.who.int/mediacentre/factsheets/fs241/en/.

15. Morris, *John*, 185–86.

16. Gary M. Burge, *John*, NIV Application Commentary (Grand Rapids: Zondervan, 2000), 115.

17. Ibid., 117.

18. Ibid., 117. Paul writes of being "adopted by God" in Romans 8. It is interesting that both the natural and the legal methods of entering a family are used as metaphors to describe our relationship to God.

19. Brenda B. Colijn, *Images of Salvation in the New Testament* (Downers Grove, IL: InterVarsity Press, 2010), 104.

20. M. Stol, *Birth in Babylonia and the Bible: Its Mediterranean Setting*, Cuneiform Monographs 14, ed. T. Abusch, et al. (Groningen: Styx, 2000), 109–10.

Chapter 5: Pain, Suffering, and Resurrection in Childbirth

1. Henry Nouwen, *The Inner Voice of Love* (New York: Image, 1998), 3.

2. There is one exception of a metaphor of painless childbirth, in Isaiah 66:7–13. In this passage, Zion gives birth before going into labor, delivering a son before the pains come upon her. "Who has ever heard of such things?" the next line remarks.

3. Before labor begins, though, be sure you discuss all the risks and benefits of various medication options with your doctor or midwife.

4. Nicky Leap, "No Pain Without Gain!," Birth International, accessed March 4, 2015, http://www.birthinternational.com/articles/midwifery/81-no-gain-without-pain.

5. Dr. Sarah J. Buckley, a medical doctor who writes excellent and well-researched articles on natural birth, offers her newsletter subscribers a free e-book, *Pain in Labour: Your Hormones Are Your Helpers*, on this topic. Alternatively, a more medically-focused report, her *Hormonal Physiology of Childbearing*, is available to read online: http://transform.childbirthconnection.org/reports/physiology/.

6. "Back labor" occurs when the baby is positioned poorly during labor and has his head in the mother's lower spine, so that it adds extra pain with each contraction. The mother feels this pain primarily in the back, not the front as in normal labor. Back labor also takes longer than normal, as it takes the baby extra time to turn correctly and navigate into the pelvis.

7. L. M. Goetzl, "Obstetric Analgesia and Anesthesia," *ACOG Practice Bulletin, Clinical Management Guidelines for Obstetrician-Gynecologists* 100, no. 36 (July 2002): 177–91. As many as 10–15 percent of women who received an epidural in childbirth report that the epidural did not provide adequate pain relief.

8. This does not apply to induced births, where contractions often come much harder and faster than natural contractions.

9. Clark and Johnson, *The Incarnation of God*, 101–02.

10. Debra Rienstra, *Great with Child: On Becoming a Mother* (La Porte, IN: WordFarm, 2008), Kindle ebook, chap. 2.

11. Hammer, *Giving Birth*, 49.

12. Epidurals, however, have been found to obliterate this oxytocin flood. C. F. Goodfellow, et al., "Oxytocin Deficiency at Delivery with Epidural Analgesia," *British Journal of Obstetric Gynaecology* 90, no. 3 (1983): 214–19.

Chapter 6: God's Providence over Pregnancy and Childbirth

1. Heidelberg Catechism, "Lord's Day 10," Canadian Reformed Theological Seminary, accessed March 3, 2015, http://www.heidelberg-catechism.com/en/lords-days/10.html.

2. Phyllis Trible, *God and the Rhetoric of Sexuality*, Overtures to Biblical Theology (Philadelphia: Fortress Press, 1978), Kindle ebook, chap. 2.

3. Sheila Kitzinger, "Obstetric Metaphors and Marketing," *BIRTH: Issues in Perinatal Care* 26, no. 1 (Mar 1999), 11.

4. In the Old Testament, infertility is assumed to be a female problem rather than a male problem. This may have been simply because in the stories included, God miraculously opens the wombs of women who cannot conceive. It is apparent that in most of these cases the husband was fertile, proven by his bearing children with servants supplied by his wife (as is the case with Sarah and Rachel) or by another wife, since polygamy was common (as in the story of Hannah).

5. Stol, *Birth in Babylonia and the Bible*, 74.

6. Abraham notes later that this was essentially true, for Sarah and Abraham had the same father, but it wasn't the whole truth (Gen 20:12).

7. Heidelberg Catechism, "Lord's Day 10," Canadian Reformed Theological Seminary, accessed February 11, 2016, http://www.heidelberg-catechism.com/en/lords-days/10.html.

8. Brother Lawrence, *The Practice of the Presence of God* (New Kensington, PA: Whitaker House, 1982), 23.

9. This passage is often used out of context to entice nonbelievers to "accept Jesus into their hearts." However, in the context of this passage, Jesus is standing at the door and knocking for the church in Laodicea, which was compromising their faith under the pressures of the Roman imperial cult and their vast wealth. Jesus promises that if anyone has ears to hear his voice and opens the door, he would come in and eat with that person.

10. Brother Lawrence, *The Practice of the Presence of God*, 6.